A Lab Report

J S Carle

First published in Great Britain in 2013
by Aberbay Publishing Limited

2nd Edition

Copyright © J S Carle 2013

J S Carle has asserted her right to be identified as the author of this work under the Copyright, Designs and Patents Act 1988.

The dogs in this book are named after the author's own dogs who inspired this book; however all other characters are fictitious and any resemblance to persons, living or dead, is purely coincidental. Places and location have been selected to help the author create a setting to allow the reader to visualise events.

This book is sold subject to the condition that it shall not, by way of trade or otherwise, be lent, copied, resold, hired out, or otherwise circulated without the publisher's prior permission, nor may it be circulated in any other form or binding than that it was originally printed and without a similar condition, including this condition, being imposed on the subsequent purchaser.

ISBN 978-0-9927017-27

Printed in Great Britain

a lab report

when I want, for the duration of her stay. They say every dog has their day. Well, I'll be having fourteen of them and intend to live every one to the 'fool' - which my human granny has been in taking on such a challenge as looking after me.

To the three C's with love

a lab report

1

In The Beginning

I like to believe I was specially selected out of my litter of thirteen but the stark reality is I was the last one remaining and not earmarked by anyone. Then a VIP call was received from Rob and Amy Maxwell asking my breeder, Mrs Maggie Brown, if there were any puppies left. She eagerly told them there was 'me'. I figured I had been left to last as I was ultra-special and nothing to do with being the runt, or possibly the brunt, of the litter. Perhaps another mitigating factor in my rejection by other potential owners was to do with my gregarious behaviour when they came to see us puppies. I so wanted to be loved I tended to lick people's faces off or, in one case of my over-zealousness, I dislodged a woman's glasses, causing them to fall to the ground and break. Arguably with her failing eyesight sight I would not have been the right dog for her anyway as I liked to run off to far flung places with little trace of my whereabouts, except perhaps some muddy paw prints. I knew Labradors who had been born to lead but I certainly wasn't one of them, unless she wanted to be led astray.

To be quite frank, I didn't want to leave Mrs Brown's. I would do whatever I could to stay in this manic family home I'd been born in to - she had five wild children, a bit like me, whom I loved to death, and three dogs (two being my Mum and Dad); what possible harm would it do to keep me? They obviously had an inkling of how I was turning out and were keen to palm me off to a good home: perhaps any home - even though I was a mere seven weeks old.

The day I met Amy and Rob will be imprinted on my mind forever. It was the day of the Royal Wedding. Prince William was marrying Kate Middleton, and rather than watch such a historic event, they had instead driven over one hundred miles from East Lothian to the bonnie, bonnie banks of Loch Lomond to meet me. This said a lot, didn't it? Or perhaps it just said they weren't fans of royalty. I liked to assume that I was, in fact, more enticing than watching such a prestigious event.

Although exceptionally knowledgeable and worldly wise for a seven week old puppy, I hadn't a clue where North Berwick was and when I had heard Mrs Brown saying to her hubby that they were coming from the sea I had a momentary panic. I had seen programmes on children's television about the sea and all

a lab report

the weird, scary creatures that lived in it, like Nessie. Oh no. I was going to be adopted by monsters. My throat dried up and I swallowed hard. I didn't want to live in or at the sea with any such creatures. I liked my house in the rolling hills, with my humongous kennel outside my owners' kitchen window and living with the little monsters I knew as 'kids'.

I tried to convince myself that I was ecstatically happy sharing my abode with my mum, dad and twelve brothers and sisters. Suddenly, the imminent prospect of leaving made me immune to my previous mumps and moans about my living conditions; the fact that my kennel stank as my doggy mum didn't seem to do much in the way of housework, probably as me and my siblings would just go and mess it up again – in one way or another if you get my drift! I would even be prepared to turn a blind eye to the cheap toys placed in our kennel for our amusement: a handle-less sweeping brush, which I thought was a household tool for sweeping up, but my insane sisters and brothers thought highly amusing to drag around with their teeth, shaking vigorously and then growling at it, before speeding off to hide behind our mum. Weird if you ask me, and indicative of future behavioural issues. I never partook in such trivial infantile play as I did not like to waste my energy on activities which did not culminate in a food reward.

My sisters and brothers were notably different from me in their approach to their attire. Some of them had nail varnish on their nails: one had pink, and he was a boy - I tried to remain very broad minded; another had neatly manicured talons with one toenail painted in a fluorescent yellow; one of my sisters even had a green toe nail on each of her front paws which made her look like she had a bad fungal infection, no doubt to be followed by her getting a verruca. The rest of the pups had an array of fancy collars on; some with glistening gold or silver name tags making them appear very posh. I learned that these decorative touches marked them out as the 'chosen' ones who had already been assigned to new owners. I had also worked out that I had none of the afore-mentioned to ear mark me but this did not perturb me in anyway - quite the opposite in fact. I did not require such cosmetic or special effects to put me in the spotlight; I was dazzling in my own right and I had convinced myself this was why Mrs Brown was doing her utmost to hold on to me as her prime pup.

I was resting in the palm of Mrs Brown's hand when the doorbell rang and, as she sprang up and walked to the door, she announced to me that the people who were waiting outside were my prospective owners and I was to be on my best behaviour; like I always wasn't! As confident as I normally was I went in to melt-down. It was now becoming all too real. I could picture it vividly. It was the monsters from twenty fathoms under the sea who awaited me and who were ready to swallow me up or cart me off to the depths of the ocean down in East Lothian. I brought my paws up to cover my eyes, curled myself in to as tight a ball as I possibly could and made sure my tail was well tucked in between my legs just in case of accidents - I had a habit of wetting myself when I got scared. My heart pounded out my chest in anticipation of what they were going to look like and I wondered if Mrs Brown would happily

a lab report

hand me over to the ogres or if she would banish them back to the sea. I hoped at least I would be included in the decision making process as I believed that I also had the right of refusal even if they wanted me. I would not be dog-napped!

Even if they were not monstrous and appeared semi-human, I still needed to establish the answers to such important questions as: Would there be kids for me to play with like in my current home and, more importantly, would there be other doggie company? Would they be able keep me to the level I was accustomed? I would not be mentioning that I was not that enamoured with my current set up if they were weirdos, as I could thole what I had if absolutely necessary. Would I have my own bed and would it be inside the house or in a wee, cold, damp, moth ridden, wooden slatted, falling apart, moss covered, no straw, NO BRUSH, kennel outside? Sorry... but I had my standards...

The door opened and I saw nothing but total darkness. Perhaps this was because I still had my eyes tightly scrunched shut with worry about what my vision would unveil. My ears were still in action though and it was via these I heard a very gentle, soft-toned voice greeting, which could have only been meant for me.

"Hello, sweet pea," she said, gliding her hand over my little black head and down across my Adonis body.

I slid my paws away from my eyes and opened them gingerly, looking slowly upwards at Amy's face. She wasn't as ugly as I'd imagined a monster to be; actually she was quite a pretty monster with her long brown hair, sallow skin and wide smile. She actually looked quite human and fairly similar to Mrs Brown. Her eyes sparkled like diamonds and I could tell she was smitten with me already. Love at first sight. Good start I thought.

Although she seemed a gentle person I knew looks could be deceiving; I wouldn't be that gullible or won over that easily without finding out a little more about her and her side kick, Rob. I was savvy enough to know my sisters and brothers looked soft and sweet but boy could they pack a punch and nip you with their wee pincers and stamp on your head as they pushed and shoved to get in to mum's milk. I had learned the art of a sharp bite back as a way to defend my teat and allocation of my milk.

Mrs Brown ushered Rob and Amy inside the house and told a fabrication of the truth to make me more of a sellable item,

'We really wanted to keep this pup for ourselves so swithered about saying she was still for sale when you phoned up to enquire."

Neatly done I thought. She went on,

"We felt that it would be good for you to come and visit her and see if you liked her and she bonded with you too."

Mrs Brown went on to explain that I was one of thirteen puppies and that my Mum (Skye), a yellow Labrador, was six years old and my Dad (Jake), a handsome black lab like myself, was four years old. Wow, Mum liked toy boys! (Like most women she had never disclosed her age to me so when Mrs Brown did, I had a wee scoff up my paw.)

At this point Maggie passed me over to Amy to have a hold of me like I was some pass-the-parcel gift at the latest kids' birthday party. Then Rob, who had come with her to drive me back to my

a lab report

new home, if I decided to go of course, asked for a 'wee shot' of me too.

I liked him; he seemed good fun as he tickled me under the chin and messed my hair up whilst referring to me as 'honey'. I fluttered my eyelashes at him being the flirt I was. I hoped Amy didn't see me as I knew she would perceive me as a challenge for his heartstrings.

Mrs Brown then led Amy and Rob, with me in hand, to my kennel out in the garden to show them my living quarters and the standard to which they would be expected to keep me. Not difficult to match I thought, unless they were going to make me sleep rough in a cardboard box. In terms of smell, that may even have been preferable to living in this large shared kennel with a netted run where thirteen pups and their mum performed their day-to-day business, which I had to pick my way through, by jumping from spot to spot, as you do when avoiding puddles, to ensure I didn't step in any poopies. My own game of hopscotch, so to put it.

Unbeknown to me at this stage, the grass was most certainly going to be greener on the other side as my new owners would be keeping me inside their house in the lap of luxury. Even my outdoor kennel in their garden was handmade, top notch and designed by an architect, with en-suite facilities and central heating. Okay, I may have let my imagination run away with me a tad: it was fitted out by the local joiner. At least not an MDF effort put together with a set of incomplete instructions, missing bolts and liable to crash down on me at the first sign of a breeze. No matter. I would spend most of my time in my owners' house and use mine for sanctuary from them. I was going to be a posh dog with two homes.

Rob bent down, with me tightly held in hand, and he and Amy spoke to my brothers and sisters by poking their fingers through the wire fencing. They remarked on their fancy collars and rainbow coloured nail varnish. I knew they thought it was weird, as I had too, and I began to warm to them even more as we seemed to be on the same wave length. For this reason it seemed fairly safe to say that if they adopted me, I wasn't going to be one of these Hollywood damsel dogs adorned with bling and make up! They also laughed aloud at my sisters and brothers sleeping on the broken brush head whilst the other ones tried to drag it around from place to place. Mrs Brown tried to justify why she had placed the brush in for us by saying that for a bitch who had whelped a lot of puppies she didn't have the capacity for them all to cuddle in to her to sleep so sweeping brush heads or toys performed a similar role and acted as good surrogates for their mum. I wanted to ask how a brush or toy produced milk but I guess no one would answer that question for me.

Mrs Brown headed back in to the kitchen with Amy and Rob and produced a copy of my pedigree line. Apparently I stemmed from a long line of 'Best in Show' champions hence my stunning good looks. I had long black eyelashes, bright amber coloured eyes, a silky black coat, a rounded head like a small football, big floppy lips and a few long whiskers under my chin (As I would discover my human granny has some whiskers under her chin too – we must have shared the same pedigree line). Mrs Brown talked about hip and eye scores which seemed like double-dutch to me and I didn't

a lab report

have a clue what she was talking about. I believe the lower the hip and eye scores Skye and Jake had the less likely I was to have any problems with my eyesight and ability to walk. Believe me - as long as I could smell my food there would be no issues!

Mrs Brown then continued with their induction on puppies by showing them the type of food she was feeding me, Beta Puppy, which translated to me as steak, fish, fresh chicken or scrambled eggs. They were told they should dilute this with a little warm distilled water to soften it up and let it all soak in for a minute or two before feeding me. Once I had eaten, my puppy belly seemed to expand about a metre and it rested on my back paws when I sat down. 'Tubby Tub' became one of the many nicknames that Amy gave me after I ate! So full of compliments was she, building my complex no end.

Further to explaining my genealogy and feeding arrangements, Maggie explained that I had been wormed (!) and that I would be due my two inoculations soonish; one at around the eight week mark and another when I reached twelve weeks old, at which point I would be ready to go out and about.

She then quizzed Amy and Rob about their experience of dogs. Amy told her that her first ever dog had been a golden Labrador named Breeze (Was it 'windy' I wondered?) and that she and Rob had two dogs at present; one was called Brambles, who had changed her name by deed poll to Bumbles as she liked eating bees. She was a Labrador/Doberman cross and they had got her from the Edinburgh Dog and Cat Home on Christmas Eve when she was just six weeks old (I heard that advert reverberate around in my head: 'A dog is for life not just for Christmas'). I had never seen a Doberman before and I wondered what she would look like. Bumbles was thirteen years old and was black like me, although going a little grey around the gills. Then there was Coco (named by Amy's nephew) who liked to think of herself as being named after the famous scent, Coco Chanel. I think I would soon see if she did smell as fragrant as the perfume or if the comment alluded to her smelling as high as a kite after rolling on a dead seagull or in some freshly passed cow dung. Coco was five years old and apparently a prime agility dog, having won quite a few trophies and rosettes. Poor dog, if she had only known I was on the way and about to eat some of her precious awards!!

Mrs Brown asked about my care arrangements as all breeders do. You see, no puppies should go to homes where people work full-time and that was especially important for me coming from Crufts' Champions!

Rob explained he worked for a multi-national insurance company in Edinburgh, which involved the odd bit of travel away from home, but Amy was at home full-time. Amy had given up teaching a few years ago in the hope of having children but so far this hadn't happened. Living with an ex-teacher was more than likely going to be a nightmare; all the rules and regulations I would be forced to follow to ensure I 'behaved appropriately at all times' and no doubt countless amounts of homework so I 'reached my full potential'. My stomach churned!

Amy remarked that I would get lots of lovely walks at the beach and round the local golf course. What was a beach? What

a lab report

was a golf course? I lived by the rolling hills with Mrs Brown, her husband and the wee yins, where I could watch the cows eat the grass and moo until their hearts were content. What would I have to watch on the beach and at a golf course? Maybe there were cows there too.

Finally... came the million dollar question. Did Amy and Rob want to take me? My ears drooped and my heart sank. If they said yes, I would be going off to a new home, on my own, with strangers, and if they said no, it was one more level of rejection. Rob held me high up in his hands and looked at me lovingly, then brought me down to his face and rubbed me against the stubble on his chin. I felt like I was back in my kennel sleeping on the brush head and I wondered if he was now going to be my new mum. He then swept his arm around Amy's shoulders, and held me closely between them. In unison, as if it had been rehearsed, both cried a unanimous...'Yes'.

My mind was sent in to orbit as thoughts whizzed through my under-developed little doggy brain. I was going to be leaving Mrs Brown, my mum, dad and my sisters and brothers. I looked at Mrs Brown and I could see tears welling up in her eyes. I was unsure if this was extreme happiness and relief at finally getting rid of pesky little me or if she was actually feeling sad and was mourning my imminent departure.

I however, had immediately turned my attention to my new owners to start some mega sooking. I gave Amy's hand a wee lick and simultaneously passed a small amount of urine into Rob's hand. Now I know some of you will be thinking I did this as a last ditch attempt to get them to refuse me, but I would never have been as manipulative as that – or would I?. Taking it all in his stride and unfazed by this action of ingratitude, he turned to Mrs Brown,

"Don't worry, puppies always do things like that."

And with that he turned on his heels and took me out in to a small enclosed area of the garden, plonked me down and encouraged me to 'go pee'. When I squeezed out what little I had left, he picked me up, gave me a quick kiss on the forehead and remarked, "Good girl." And that's how I learned to get my treats for the next few months.

After saying goodbye to the kids, Mrs Brown and her hubby, Skye, Jake and all my brothers and sisters, I headed off to my new home in East Lothian. I was to be cuddled by Amy for the duration of the journey in the back seat of Rob's estate car. As Maggie waved us off I felt a compounding yet conflicting mixture of emotions which ranged from angst to excitement. I had new owners who really wanted me, but would miss my family who I'd spent seven fun yet crazy weeks with. I sought refuge in Amy's fleecy jacket, burying my head deep into its warmth and made little whimpering noises as I did so. This forced her to cuddle me even closer and stroke my coat until I felt overwhelmingly tired and fell asleep about ten minutes in to the journey. I didn't rouse until the car came to rest in the driveway of my new home – without 'going pee' at any stage of my deep sleep.

a lab report

2

Settling In To My New Home

Have you ever seen 'Who Let the Dogs Out'? Well, I was about to partake in one of their unprecedented offline programmes! I was lifted out the car by Amy, still semi-comatose from my mammoth two hour journey, and taken safely in through the front gate. Through my half shut eyes, I scanned the garden as best I could with my developing vision - I was still a little short sighted at this age. I clocked a rockery, full of beautiful flowering plants. There was also a vast open green space, lined by high hedging with a tree in the middle of the lawn. Suddenly the urge to 'go pee' overtook me - puppies and the elderly have a lot in common on awakening: Amy just managed to put me down on the grass in the nick of time, as I let go of my cascading river. A second later and that fleecy blanket she had been encasing me in, which now smelt like burnt toast (puppies always do), would have been the worse for wearing – with me! I sniffed where I had just wet and Amy praised me remarking I was a 'clever girl' for doing that (or was it for me going for a pee – who knows?) and I got another small treat for performing a routine procedure. Food, glorious food.

All quiet on the western front and no sign of my new family yet. Amy had picked me back up and was carrying me in her left hand. As I was still pint sized I fitted neatly on her palm, with my legs dangling down at either side of it. I really was 'cutesy'.

With her free hand, she was now turning a key in the front door and pushing it open. Instantly, two big black noses were pressed up against the glass on the internal door. The dogs were wagging their tails in excitement, or anticipation at their new house-mate, and their whole bodies were gyrating to the rhythm.

Amy opened the door and they jumped up and down like Jack-in-the-boxes to see her and vie for her attention, until that was... they clapped eyes on me. I thought only cars could hit a reverse gear but both Bumbles and Coco seemed to be able to do exactly that. Amy placed me down in the hall, near them but not beside them, if you know what I mean. Within their vicinity perhaps would be a better way to describe it. She then proceeded to do the formal introductions, in a deliberate tone,

"This is Rosie. She is your new sister and she's here to stay."

I looked at them, they looked at me, I looked at them, and they looked at me. This routine seemed to hang in space until

a lab report

Bumbles about turned and retreated to the garden in what seemed like utter contempt and an 'I've been through all this before' look. Coco seemed marginally more inquisitive, sniffing me all over then did, what I now refer to, as her 'Elvis impression' which involved her curling up her lip at one side - uh, uh, uh, yeah, yeah, yeah - frighteningly funny! She followed this up by giving me a big barky growl right in my face as if to stipulate 'don't mess with me midget gem'. She then bid me adieu and headed out to the garden to join forces with the bee catcher. Rob followed Coco and Bumbles whilst I pranced behind Amy in to the kitchen - what would become my favourite room in the house (I am now the official Sous-Chef) and observed her unpacking my puppy food. She then lifted a big pink girly doggy bowl up from the 'assigned feeding area of the kitchen' and put a few handfuls of my food in to it. After soaking it in a little water, as Mrs Brown had advised, she put it down, in front of my nose, to enable me to have my first feed in my new abode.

No chance of getting straight in there though as Amy already had delusions of grandeur and pushed my hind legs in to a seated position, holding me in a wait for a few seconds before allowing me to get tore in. That sitting and waiting added a whole two seconds to my ten seconds eating time. Labs are notoriously greedy and fast eaters, with us puppies being even quicker – you snooze, you lose in the puppy world!

With my swingingly full belly, that looked as though I had a horrendously bad bout of IBS, and significant deposits of my food still clinging to my face and whiskers, I headed out to the garden to make friends with my new sisters. I did however let Amy lead the way and apparently coax me out to make myself look ultra-cool at the same time as doing my best to feign disinterest. Coco boss – sure! Maybe for today. Once I had my paws under the table there would be no quibbles about who was in charge.

    I set my first paw in to the back garden; more bushes and fruit trees - yum. It was a stiflingly hot day and I really didn't want to lie and bake in it as too much sun on a young coat is not a good thing and may dye my hair grey as had happened to my human granny. I therefore opted to lie just inside the back door on a stack of towels, which I later found out were for drying us wet dogs on return from walks. The breeze made me feel sleepy and off I drifted, imagining I was the gatekeeper to the house and Coco and Bumbles would have to plead with me, by offering me reams of food, to let them back in.

    Flash, flash, flash. My eyes sprang open to see Rob poised behind a Nikon D50 with 55-200mm lens. I had been moved from my cosy pile of towels to a wooden floor and was sized up alongside one of Amy's slippers, which stank of cheesy feet; mine were probably no better.

    I understood the need to capture my iridescent beauty to submit to the latest edition of Horse and Hound but I had barely been here a few hours. I stretched, just to prove I was longer than the smelly slipper, yawned and stumbled to my feet. I was just stepping over it when I let flow with the most massive pee imaginable. Rob whisked me up, and ran through the hallway to the backdoor and straight in to the garden. I had left a lovely dribbly trail in my wake - similar to those water planes do when trying to

a lab report

extinguish bush fires. Rob plonked me on the grass and I looked up at him wistfully, knowing I was all but done. I wondered off, sniffed a bush or two and then let some squidgy stuff come out from under my tail. I sniffed it too; what a beautiful perfume it had.

Rob called my name, "Rosie."

I was totally unfamiliar with this as 'my name' and he started tapping the side of his leg as he tried to cajole me into the house – which I complied with as I reckoned that it must be about feeding time. Well, that was a pup's routine; eat, sleep, pee and poo and I had done the latter two, so we were back to number one. As I chirpily bounded through the hallway I was met, at eye level, by Amy who seemed to be dipping some sort of cloth in to a basin of antiseptic-smelling water. She obviously had some sort of OCD given she was doing housework at this time of night (6pm)! I flew past her and followed Rob in to the kitchen and saw him lift up that loveable pink dish of mine and fill it with my food. I burled round and round on the spot in sheer anticipation. Seconds passed and I was becoming more impatient and was now dancing on the spot, paws going ten to the dozen as he mixed in my water. Next thing I knew Bumbles and Coco were by my side, giving me the evil eye. I saw two other dishes being filled by Rob, with copious amounts of brown pellets and then he mixed in some fishy smelling stuff called tuna which came from a container in the fridge. Although mine was a smaller looking bowl it was piled higher than theirs so I flashed them a quick smile of one-upmanship.

"Sit," commanded the boss with the food.

Coco and Bumbles put their bottoms on the tiled floor; I

continued to dance. Bumble's bowl was made of metal and Rob placed this in a high holder, well out of my reach, for her to eat from as she was a tall dog. Coco's bowl was placed on the floor in front of her and had a heavy looking orange ball in it, which I believe prevents her from scoffing her food, gulping air and doing a hefty burp afterwards. Not very polite! As her bowl was at my level I took the opportunity to chance my arm and ran forward, guzzling as much as I could before Rob pushed my nose out of it, pinched me by the scruff and moved me out of harm's way, allowing Coco in to her own bowl to feed. My bowl was then swiftly placed in front of me so I could start demolishing my own nosh. As my interest was now fully focused on my eats, Rob said 'go' to the other two, by which time I was just finishing mine and heading over to Coco's for seconds. Coco looked up from her bowl and gave me her best smile; I could see all of her front teeth and very nice and white they were too; she must use the extra whitening toothpaste. Just as I took a dip into the bowl, I was airlifted by Rob and placed outside the kitchen door, which was then abruptly shut in my face. Très rude! I pressed my nose off the glass to show my level of disapproval and left some nice snot marks on the window which ended up obscuring my view as they made it foggy.

    Amy had just finished cleaning the hall carpet behind me and was now putting something down all over the carpet and tiles; I'll give you a clue – it's black and white and read all over – yip, newspaper. Great I thought; a licence to pee and poop anywhere. She then returned the spare newspapers to the basement and I sat at the top of the stairs watching her. She told me to stay on

a lab report

the 'top step' and I got a 'Good girl' for doing so and a minuscule treat out of her trouser pocket. After flicking the basement light off she gathered me up in her arms and took me through to the living room to watch the tv with her. I lay across her tummy, on my back, and she stroked my bald belly, calling me 'Tubby, Tub' as it was inflated like a helium balloon and not looking like it would deflate anytime in the near future unless I passed some air (or a silent suffocator as I called them - always done around someone else so I never got the blame). Warm, cosy and petted, I was soon in the land of nod again.

"O F T L T," I heard Rob say loudly, at the same time as the television was being switched off. Bumbles and Coco sprang to their feet from their black rug in front of the coffee table and ran out the living-room, through the hallway and out through a magical hole, with pretend glass in it, in the back door. Now your guess is as good as mine as to what the acronym meant, but they seemed to know. **O**ff **T**he **B**lack **M**at; it wasn't that. **O**ff **F**or **T**v **L**ate **T**ime; that didn't sound right either. Then it hit me, **O**ut **F**or **T**he **L**ast **T**ime. What a bright, intelligent puppy I was. I could be studying applied acronyms at Oxford at the age of seven weeks beating the record of the youngest ever student. Just as I was mulling my greatness over Amy picked me up and carried me to the back door, opened the dog flap with her left hand and stuck me through it with her right one, placing me on the decking. SCAREY. It was dark and I am out here alone with Bubby (my new name for her) and Coco. I am sure I would be able to navigate my whereabouts using Coco's fluorescent smile!

I wandered over towards Coco and walked underneath her belly to search for some much needed milk. I was parched. Coco smiled at me again; I knew then our friendship was developing. Bubby was further over in the garden and was eating grass like I'd seen the cows do back in my Trossachs' home. I sidled up near her and joined in; she didn't seem to mind me being there as long as I respected her personal space of a least a few metres radius in all directions. Suddenly a light sprang on from the side of the house. I looked at Bubby, and she continued chewing the cud, so I guessed there was nothing for me to worry about. I learned later on that it was just the security light.

I looked back towards the door and I saw Rob and Amy watching me, so I waved to them. Okay I am fibbing. I then squatted down, passed some liquid and headed back to the flap. Coco and Bubby tore through it, smashing their heads off the glass type panel and flinging their legs and body through it - leaving me behind. Just as I was thinking Amy and Rob had forgotten I existed, a hand reached through the flap, gathered me up and whipped me through. Off to the kitchen again I thought. Great. We were lined up on the tiles like a firing line and given three suppertime biscuits each. I just got mine for being pushed in to a seated position for each one – easy, peasy, lemon squeezy! Coco and Bubby had to do tricks for theirs like performing clowns. High fives, guess the hand and a lie down. Coco then took a long drink of water out the bowl beside our empty food dishes. Being a Pavlova puppy I copied her; or should that have been Pavlov? I knew one was an animal psychologist and the other a Russian Ballerina, or

a lab report

was it a creamy meringue? I did get confused at times as my brain tried to process my wealth of knowledge. Anyway in order for me to reach it I had to climb up on the edge of the bowl to get to the wet stuff as I was so wee. Once I had finished I moved back along the kitchen tiles, leaving another wet line marking my travels; at least this one could be allowed to dry of its own accord. Amy and Rob laughed at me.

"Bedtime," they said in harmony.

Coco and Bubby headed through to the study and I followed behind them. Their beds were plush and furry lined; they reeked expense. They stepped in them and burled round and round, flattening what would have been grass if they had been wild dogs sleeping rough. Watching them made me feel quite nauseous. Eventually they settled in to curled-up balls, pressing their backs around the edges of the beds. I was just about to take a running jump to join Coco in hers when Amy gathered me up saying, "Let sleeping dogs lie". I thought they couldn't tell lies if they were sleeping so what a silly phrase to come out with.

I was then transported in my human helicopter and taken up a 'flight' of stairs to the bedroom on the left of the top 'landing'. As I rounded the corner I clapped eyes on this palatial sized bed dressed in five hundred thread count Egyptian cotton sheets. Most would be impressed by that alone but as I am not shallow or materialistic I had a keener eye for 'George the cuddly monkey' nestled between the pillows at the headboard. He was just crying out for me to rescue him and chomp his little fat monkey cheeks. Amy, oblivious to my intentions, lifted me up and placed me on the bed for what she thought was keeping me out of harm's way. It took me a whole nano–second to reach George.

I had just got my tiny milk teeth in to his black triangular nose when I felt a firm nip of my scruff and I was being airlifted by Rob, in a steep descent, to a navy and light blue tartan, oval shaped bed underneath their bedroom window. Sub-standard I thought; no furry blanket and the base was foam. It was also about twenty million times too big for a seven week old pup and was more suited to a fully grown Great Dane. I would just like to reiterate that I am not materialistic but I did have standards and I could tell that this bed was neither new nor expensive like my sisters' ones downstairs. Even the tooth marks around the top told me that this was second hand. Sleep in this I thought; what a cheek – I was from a long list of show winning pedigrees (even if one had a pedigree name that had Rogue Trader as part of it)! There were no toys in it or a brush. I would be sleeping rough! I sat bolt upright in the bed in protest but neither of them seemed to notice as they got changed in to their night clothes. Revenge is a dish best served cold and that was exactly how I would deal with this situation.

Rob came over and patted me on top of my head, "Goodnight pup, sleep well and use the newspaper if you need to go pee during the night."

Amy held my little podgy face in her hands, kissed my forehead and said, "Night Rosie, and sweet dreams in your new home." She then returned to bed, pulled the covers across them both and switched out the light.

I drifted off to dreamy land, lips and feet twitching as I ran

a lab report

through the meadows chasing butterflies.

    I must have woken around 3am. It was still dark outside and there was a snorting, choking sound radiating from Rob's side of the bed that sounded like some monster creeping around the room. I must be at the sea after all and Nessie was here to guard me and ensure I stayed put. I screwed up my eyes and scanned the room. No sign of any creatures or ghouls. I then listened for a moment or two before I plucked up the courage to step out of my bed. I skipped across the newspaper and squatted for a gargantuan pee at Rob's side of the bed; they would never know I'd done it there as by morning it would all be dried in. It was a natural wood floor and I knew from my scientific background that the burns from ammonia would take at least three weeks or more to turn the wood black and out me. Revenge and all that! I then took one of these freaky mad turns to myself and lolloped back to the newspaper, flung myself to the ground, rolling around on it and flicking it up with my paws, at the same time as seeing how much I could get in to my mouth to chew.

    Suddenly, I froze. Rob had pulled the duvet back and was about to step out the side of the bed. Gulp! One foot, two foot, wet under there. Flicking the light on quickly at his bed side he looked down at the pool of urine engulfing his feet like a warm water bath. He looked over at me and I don't think I saw any smile radiate from his lips on this occasion. He kept his eyes firmly on me as he stood up. I continued to look non-plussed and now rolled on to my side; newspaper trailed out the side of my mouth and I imagined I looked very fetching in the low light. Rob must have had sore feet as he walked on his heels as he moved towards the little newspaper left unshredded on the floor beside me. He then proceeded to walk flat footed back and fore on it until there no longer appeared to be any wet footprints. Very strange. Moving towards the seat he reached out over my head and pulled on a fleece and woolly hat. He had a pair of lounge trousers on already; which was just as well as I was too young to witness nudity. The silence was deafening and I felt out of my comfort zone with his lack of conversation. He slid his hand underneath my oxsters and tucked me inside his fleece for the journey down the stairs.

On reaching the back door, he opened up the dog flap and then popped me out through it and I was left staring back at him from outside. A head then appeared through the flap with the instruction to 'go pee'. I had nothing left in me so I just sat where I was and faked shivering so I would be lifted back in. Just at this point I was flung to the decking floor as Coco and Bubby came pelting out the flap at the rate of noughts. Coco raced to the old cattle sink and gulped down the cold water, which also seemed to have a toad jumping about in the bottom of it. Bubby started to bark to let the neighbourhood know she was alive and kicking. I seemed invisible to both (not invincible as I would become in the future).

"Right you lot – in!" Rob shrieked from a now opened door.

Coco and Bubby ran in past him and straight back to their beds and I followed like some lost lamb having just missed being slaughtered for my show earlier on. I was taken back upstairs and literally dumped back in my Scottish-themed bed. After a quick mop of the floor, at his side of the bed, with some toilet tissue and

a lab report

wipes, Rob peeled off his fleece and hat and threw them on the chair beside me. However in his haste he failed to notice that the woolly hat had fallen in to my bed so I pounced on it quickly to hide it from his view. He crept back in to bed, drew the covers back over himself, switched the light off, and within minutes was snoring deeply. I however was hard at work making a designer hat for Amy which would have a special hole in it for women with pony tails.

I must have drifted off at some point as the next thing I remember was Amy opening the blinds and reaching in to my bed and holding up my night's work.

"Rob... you know your favourite cosy woolly hat... well... it may not be anymore."

I smiled proudly at my achievements and even though she seemed to be giggling at the point of showing it to him, I got a 'bad dog' comment from her seconds later. I couldn't think of anything I'd just done in the last few seconds that merited that comment. After all, the hat demolition, or I prefer to call it 'reconstruction,' had been hours ago, or even days ago in the life of a dog as we aged at seven years for every human year. The comment therefore fell on deaf ears and I was already plotting my next line of action.

I lunged at Amy's bare feet, nipping and licking her toes. She laughed hysterically at the same time as scanning the room for her pink knitted slippers to put on. Rob was sitting up by now watching me in action and smiling again – thank goodness. Once her slippers were on I used my teeth to grab on to the back of them as she walked so I got pulled along on my belly. This was a game I loved and continued to play for the next three months, at which point I got too heavy for her to be able to drag me anymore. My motto was, and still is: if it moves along the floor, pounce on it, grab it, bark or growl at it and failing all, chew it up and eat it. Equally, if it doesn't move, chew it up and eat it. Just eat it!

As I'll tell you later on, some of my exploits have proved very interesting and even airport security would have difficulty outing my smuggling techniques; which may make me a prime candidate for MI5. I am the epitome of Lab puppies and admirably demonstrate our quest for living life to the full at all times. I am also proof that what goes in, most often comes out but not necessarily in its original form!

a lab report

3

Day Two Onwards

It was my first morning here at my coastal abode and after the hat fiasco and slipper ride I had been transported down to the first level by my Stannah chairlift, called Rob. I was immediately posted out the flap to join Coco and Bubby in the garden. This was to enable me to visit the ladies, or to empty my tank as they say, to create space for the fuel I was about to eat called 'breakfast'.

I wandered round the garden and looked for a space to do my business. I spotted Coco near the Silver Birch tree and Bubby at the opposite corner beside the bay tree. Both were squatting and brown piles of stuff exuded from beneath their tails, which they bolted away from instantly they finished. It seemed to steam in the cold air and I watched with interest until I got a passing whiff my way, which made me choke on the rancid fumes and sent me careering across the garden to a safe haven. My own squidgy stuff was pleasantly pungent but I drew the line at second hand stuff, as you know already! Coco and Bubby had now vanished in to the house via the flap and I was left hanging about outside on my own again. This seemed to be a recurring theme. I meandered over to the flap, hauled myself up and managed to get my front paws up on to the lower rim of its opening. I stuck my nose against the flap and head-butted it enough to prise it open a small way. I then tried to flick one of my back legs up on to the same ledge as my front paws but ended up swimming in mid-air as I was suspended half in and half out, balancing on my belly. I must have been there for what felt like ages before Rob spotted me from the dining room.

"Quick, come and look at this!" he bellowed to Amy.

She came racing through to join him and they both stood laughing at me. After taking the mickey out of me for a few minutes, Rob came through, pushed the flap wide open and lifted me in and proceeded to turn me over to see my badly scraped bald belly caused by being hung, drawn and quartered for the last few minutes. I would need to be cared for now given my level of injuries and Rob tried to soothe and heal the pain by giving me a kiss directly on my sores. Once placed down on the floor I raced through, at break-neck speed, like a battered formula one car, to the kitchen where my pink dish was waiting for me alongside Coco and Bubby's. Amy made us all sit again… I sat back on my heels so she could notice the scrapes on my belly, enticing her to take pity

a lab report

on me. As my belly wasn't full of food yet my injuries were less visible, so my attention seeking ploy failed on this occasion.

One by one, and starting with bossy Bubby, we were released from our seated position to eat our breakfast. Once told to 'go on' I launched my face in to my dish like a child dooking for apples and never drew breath until the last morsel was gone. Lick, lick, double lick just in case I'd missed anything.

I was first finished, again, and made a 'beeline' for Bubby's high dish which I would do my best to climb up to (now that I'd nearly managed the flap the world was my oyster). Bubby stopped, stared at me with a look which spelt out D A N G E R so I swiftly spun round and headed for pushover Coco's dish. She'd just finished up so I stepped right in to the dish itself and flicked the orange ball around with my nose as I licked up the remaining crumbs. Stepping back out of the dish, I started pushing it ferociously across the floor, like there was no tomorrow, until it wedged itself against the kitchen units and I could have one last lick round the inside and outside of it. When I looked up I had food strewn across my eyebrows, along the sides of my floppies, on my forehead and all over the top of my head. Amy laughed in dismay and told me that there was no way I would be eating out anywhere fancy until my manners had improved somewhat. I was what she referred to as 'making a real dogs dinner' of eating my food. She then gathered up the dishes and placed all three in the sink. What a liberty I thought - I hadn't licked out Bubby's yet.

Amy poured herself a cup of tea, put her fleece and matching woolly hat on (that would be matching Rob's woolly hat that was now a 'has been') and we all returned to the garden again. The air was cold and I shivered a little as I still only had my thin puppy coat on. I decided the best way to heat up was to liven things up so I bounded over to Coco and ran underneath her stomach. She tried to reach down to nip me as I played 'In and Out the Dusting Bluebells' with her legs. This really got her dander up and eventually she tried to flatten me by flopping on top of me to crush every last ounce of air out of me and leave me looking like one of these dead animal fur carpets; though given my current size I'd probably have been more appropriately used as a hot water bottle cover or pyjama case. I clambered up on her and sat proudly along her side; I called it playing horsy, horsy.

With little time to reflect on my victory she flipped on to her back and using all four paws, tossed me high in to the air like some acrobatic ball. The last thing I remembered was landing full pelt in the hedge and dangling from some branches. I spotted Bubby along from me on the grass acting nonchalantly, but I could tell she was acutely amused by what she had just witnessed; the sadist! It was a moment or two before I dropped back to earth of my own accord and I chose to cut my losses and head straight back in to the house, away from the gruesome twosome, before I could be bullied any more. It was tough being the new dog on the block.

I found Amy and Rob sitting in the dining room eating their breakfast and chatting. I lay across Amy's feet and looked up at her with my cupboard love eyes. Any morsel dropping on the floor would be mine to hoover up and I was more than happy to assist with keeping floors crumb free. Who needed an expensive

a lab report

Dyson when dogs like me could do the same job for free and in half the time? I should start my own franchise... Now, there was a thought... for another day when I was bored... and therefore unlikely to happen as I could always find something to amuse me.

I heard a scraping of bowls and it appeared that both Amy and Rob had finished and no crumbs had fallen my way at all. Just when I was thinking game's a bogie - not on the kitchen door's window this time - she reached down and gave me a cornflake. I gnashed it out of her hand and chomped on it for ages as it started to stick like toffee to my teeth and the roof of my mouth as it got soggy. I rolled about on the floor, rubbing my face along it to try and dislodge it but no can do. Eventually Amy had to pull me up on to her lap, open my mouth wide like some dentist and remove the offending obstacle. She then ate it herself. Only joking... she stuck it in her dish which was about to head for the dishwasher. After she had assembled the plates from the table and left Rob reading the morning newspaper, which was multi-purpose and doubled as my night time toilet paper, she headed through to the kitchen. I traced her every slipper step. She loaded the dirty dishes in to the dishwasher and I took the opportunity, as any dog would, to lick the plates in it that were nearest me before my face was pushed off and the door closed. That was another job my franchise could offer: plate cleaning.

A wide smirk spread across my face as I remembered an old joke about a wee boy visiting his grand-dad and remarking on the traces of the egg yolks from breakfast still being on the dinner plates. His grand-dad had told him cold water had got them clean as cold water could, so just to get on and eat off them; that they were as clean as could be. On leaving that night to go home the little boy had been met by a barking dog which he was too frightened to go past in case it bit him. He had retreated to his grand-dad's, who then came to the front door and shouted, "Cold Water, come on in." I know that if his grand-dad had employed me there would not have been any egg yolk traces left on them there plates so Cold Water should have been sacked!

Amy was now in the bathroom and I nudged open the door to see what she was up to. She had a towel wrapped around her and was using some sort of implement which made a brrrr…ing noise on her teeth. She looked in the mirror at the same time and she reminded me of how Coco looked when she smiled at me; lots of lovely white pegs. She then ditched the towel and stepped in to some weird looking Tardis which I believe to be a shower cubicle. It had rain running down the inside of the glass and I pressed my nose and face up against it and did my best to lick it dry. Amy disappeared behind some fog and we seemed to lose each other for five minutes or so, until the Tardis door re-opened and a Dalek climbed out. I looked Amy up and down; she had a bald belly like mine - she was actually quite bald all over except for some fur dotted here and there. She must get cold in winter I thought and this helped me understand the need for humans to wear these funny looking garments over their bodies.

I observed her drying herself and putting some white stuff on her face that made her look like a geisha girl until it had fully dried in. She then used this stick thing and rolled it about under

a lab report

her armpits; that would have made me giggle and roll about on my back if it had been me. Then she squeezed some creamy stuff out of a holder on to her hands, rubbed them together and spread it all over her skin, massaging it in. I ran over and started licking her legs; the exfoliating properties of my tongue could not be underestimated. She pushed me away saying, "Stop licking my legs," so I just moved on to her hands. What weird habits these humans have I thought. All that attention lavished on no coat and having to apply conditioner every day to try and grow some protective hair like mine... what an effort. Whereas me, I had one coat, rain or shine, which was good to go for all occasions.

I was now back in the bedroom and in my classy tartan bed. Not. Rob had also had his shower and both were dressing for the day ahead. As it was a Saturday Rob wasn't dashing away to work so they had planned to take us all out for a long walk. Coco and Bubby had their collars put on. Coco's was pink with diamonds inset on sapphires and Bubby's was rubies and diamonds interspersed on black leather. Did I tell you I have a vivid imagination? Coco's was a bright red collar with pictures of luminous silver bones round it. It had a fancy buckle bone fastening and silver and red name tag on it with her mobile phone number on it. I was well impressed that she had her own mobile. Bubby's collar was purple and had both her name and mobile number embroidered on it – very posh! I had this thin red collar placed around my neck which had a little bell on it. It had a few chew marks out of it too so, I am guessing, like with the bed, this wasn't bought specifically with me in mind either! Hand me downs were the name of the day and I had certainly been on the receiving end of two in the last twenty-four hours. Just not good enough… just not.

The golf course was surprisingly devoid of players for a Saturday morning, which was normally peak time for those people who liked to spoil a nice walk by hacking round the course. I peeked out of Rob's fleece to see a wide open expanse of green grass which was much bigger than my garden. There were funny bits of material on sticks dotted around the place which blew back and fore in the wind. By my reckoning, there seemed to be a number of beaches here too, all with fierce metal pronged rakes on them; not as soft and gentle looking as my brush head back in the Trossachs. Bubby and Coco had run off in to the horizon and Rob took the opportunity to extract me from his cosy top and lower me down on to the fairway (even though at the tender age of seven weeks and a day and no inoculations, he really shouldn't have been doing so as I was unprotected from all these nasty doggie viruses that lurk around such as 'Pablo' Virus).

I dropped to my bottom and sat for a second or two admiring what little view I had from my enormous height of 20cm or so; I could see Rob and Amy's shoes, grass and then some higher grasses which towered over me; 'ruff' I think they called it. I would soon learn that the rough was where I would use my killer hunting nose to suss out golfers' lost balls and race with these to my owners for a reward of some treats. Sometimes on a good day I would even manage to find four or five and the quality and newness of the balls, I discovered, merited different levels of superiority of treat. Another franchise for me I wondered? Once my mind had

a lab report

stopped wandering and reality came back in to focus, I took to my feet and cantered for a few metres and came to a squatting stop for a pee. I received a 'Good girl' comment and a tiny treat from them for the pleasure of watching me. It was amazing that my urinating provided so much entertainment for my human owners.

Rob ran ahead of me and beckoned on me to chase him. I looked bemused but played along anyway to feed his ego. I was puggled after a minute of two and sat down for a breather. A moment later Coco and Bubby were back at my side and Amy gathered me in to the palm of her hand as we continued our walk. As my sweaty coat dried and the wind whipped up she placed me in her snuggle down 12.5 tog jacket, along with all the goose and duck down feathers. I could feel a sneeze coming on.... Atishoo! Amy and Rob laughed at me and as they had ridiculed me I chose to rub my little snotty black nose all over the inside of Amy's jacket as pay back. Soon after I was so warm and cosy I fell asleep and don't remember anything else until I woke up in front of the fire in the living room.

It was one o'clockish and it was lunch time – food! Wise to my incontinence problem on my awakening, I was scooped up by Amy and fired out to the garden and placed in the wilderness with the playground thugs, Bubby and Coco, to do the proverbial numbers one and two. It took me about forty seconds to relieve myself and complete the given tasks, with a 'Clever girl' from Amy as she watched me. Did she not have any concept as to how embarrassing it was to have my ablutions analysed? I smiled remembering that I had seen Amy starkers earlier on that day in the bathroom so perhaps I was in no place to remark on such things. I hadn't however seen her shoogle her bottom to free herself of any drips and flick her feet behind her to cover her scent. Nope, she had the Andrex puppy, soft as a baby's bottom toilet paper to soothe her and a flush that got rid of all the nasty business that us dogs had to eat out the latrines in the good old days. I wondered why they were referred to as the 'good old days' as most of the tasks that we'd had to do seemed pretty dog darn awful to me. Anyway, I thought, why am I thinking about such repulsive, stomach churning issues when I should be filling my tummy with my soggy food? I was ravishing for my food (did that mean the same as ravenous? I was never very good with my synonyms, acronyms, anyfings).

I took to my heels, with Bubby and Coco close behind me, and bolted like Usain through to the kitchen. Rob let me fly through the glass door before quickly flicking it with his foot to shut out the raging monsters behind me. There was after all only one pink bowl sitting in the middle of the floor and that had only my name on it. Only puppies such as 'moi' got fed three times daily. Coco and Bubby would just have to watch me guzzle my food down and drool in hope of me leaving something behind; not on your nelly duff would that ever happen unless I collapsed and died half way through eating it. Given I was young and vital that was so... unlikely. As soon as my bowl hit the deck I lunged forward and buried my head in my food.

Rob grasped me gently by the tail and pulled me back. Resistance training at such a young age. I pulled forward with all my might but made no impression in terms of getting

a lab report

anywhere near my bowl. "Sit," demanded Rob. I had just done that in the garden I thought. It came again, even more forcefully. "Sit," and on this occasion my bottom was pushed to the floor and my hind legs folded under it like some coiled spring; I managed to just keep my derrière off the cold slate tiles as I didn't want to catch piles. They would make pooping even more of a strain and with my IBS belly that could be a disastrous combination! I looked up at Rob's face and after playing statues for a count of five seconds he released me on a 'go on' command to my bowl. After a few quick mouthfuls to stave off my hunger I angled myself further round the bowl so I could see Bubby and Coco through the glass door and I could eat facing them. I picked little bits out of my bowl and emulated the cows chewing the cud near my home in the Trossachs. I looked up at them between mouthfuls so I could help tantalise their taste buds as they watched me savour every moment. Taunting I think it's called. When I finally finished I spent some time licking in and around the bowl. Nothing left at all for these greedy bitches. Hee, hee. Bending down, Rob lifted up my squeaky clean dish. If it had been metal like Bubby's bowl he would have been able to see his reflection in it; just as well it wasn't otherwise I may have tried to eat myself. I got a pat on the head from Rob and he smiled,

"What a good girl you are. You must know there aren't any famished puppies round here who are going to steal your food anymore so you could take your time over it."

I grinned from ear to ear; not quite my motive for eating slowly but no need for him to know that. I wagged my tail to show my gratitude. I appreciated the fact that he talked to me like I understood what he was saying. Which I did of course; not that I could ever let on as that would blow my cover.

The next few days were pretty similar. I continued the need to 'go pee' during the night but given my boredom levels as all my compadres slept, I decided to amuse myself as part of the process. Immediately I felt the need to pass liquid I would eject myself from my bed to afford myself a generous amount of time to peruse the newspaper on the floor. I wasn't looking for an intellectually stimulating article to read or a crossword to complete as I sat on the toilet seat like I believe many men do when they spend hours in the bathroom. Nope, I was looking for the ugliest face ever to go to print; please remember at this point that beauty is in the eye of the beholder and we may disagree on this front. I awarded myself a full ten points for a drowning or five points for partially submersing. I always managed to score highly where Clifford the Dog or that immensely annoying Scooby Dooby Doo were involved; one has to question what sort of a name that is, even if it is a triple barrelled one like my Kennel Club one, 'Kenmillix Kleptomaniac Rogue'.

Having run out of ugly mutts by night four I became, what my owners termed, 'house trained'. That really only applied to night time as during the day when I was in the house I would feel the urge to go and although I would make an attempt to reach the flap, inevitably I would crouch somewhere en route to make my puddle. I quite liked the feeling of the warm liquid as my toes sunk into the squidgy bit of carpet. I would jump about in it afterwards

a lab report

like a child in a puddle with their wellies on. When I saw Rob or Amy heading towards me I'd take to my heels, quick as a flash and hurtle, at high speed through the flap, like a dog running from a crime scene. With the police team in close pursuit, I'd position myself behind a tree so Amy and Rob couldn't catch me. It took both of them and the use of a garden chair to block me off before I was captured. I was then marched back to the scene, placed beside it and told 'Bad dog' before being stuck out in the garden again. Being told 'Bad dog' had no effect on me whatsoever as you will know as us dogs have no moral conscience, so Rob should have saved his breath. What an energy he expended on such a trivial mishap I thought. Does Amy go and fetch Rob every time there is a splash on the tiles around the toilet? I don't think so. Next time I'll just make it to the dining room tiles then and there should be no complaints or it will be a case of the pot calling the kettle black!

j s carle

4

Eight Weeks Old

It was now Tuesday, the start of the eleventh day in my new home and a momentous occasion as I turned eight weeks old. I had pictured in my mind's eye a humongous birthday cake with eight bone shaped biscuits waiting for me to gnaw off the top layer, or alternatively, eight bone-shaped candles for me to extinguish with some gases expelled from my derrière which would certainly start my party with an explosion. It would also have the desired effect of ensuring Coco and Bubby would be less keen to sink their gnashers in to it and steal a piece.

Rob had followed the usual morning routine of extraditing us to the garden at six am for the all-important acts. With the

a lab report

excitement of my pending feast, fit for a queen, I performed these quicker than you could say 'Happy Birthday to the greatest dog on earth' and, hyper-ventilating with anticipation, pelted through to the kitchen to see what gourmet breakfast awaited me in my pink bowl. I peered at it in disbelief. No cake. No special treat? Have you forgotten what day this is? I looked up at Rob in utter disgust and bent my head down to my bowl, munched a bit of my food then spat it out on the floor. I repeated this action until a little pile had accumulated. Rob was now starting to look concerned. "Got ya," I thought, so I continued with my Oscar award nominee performance.

"Why you not eating your food, pup?" Rob asked in a concerned voice.

I stuck my tongue out in a sickly sort of way.

"Amy!" Rob shouted. "Rosie must have an upset tummy or something as she's not eating her food this morning. What should I do?"

Minutes later I heard Amy descending the staircase and appear next to me in the kitchen.

"What's wrong with you this morning my little furry friend?"

I gave her the big puppy eyed, sorrowful, woe-is-me look.

"She's too young to know that we are going to the vet today so that's not going to put her off her food, is it?" she quizzed Rob.

"Not unless Coco and Brambles have been winding her up…. but as dogs can't talk, I think that is highly unlikely."

What's the vet I pondered? They were so far off track they were almost hypothermic I thought. Just at that point my tummy made a massive gurgling noise and Amy laughed.

"Well, by the sound of that she's hungry so let's just make her some scrambled eggs and rice just in case she has a dickie tummy. I can get the vet to check her when we go later anyway."

So there they were, preparing a special birthday meal for me. Typically, like other posh restaurants, I had to wait two minutes and thirty seconds as the microwave worked its magic with the ingredients. With a little milk added to cool it, my flamingo coloured dish was lowered to the floor and 'cause I wasn't well' I wasn't even made to sit before digging in. I ate slowly so as not to give the game away too much and when finished, even received some praise. The little mound of my regurgitated food from earlier was still on the floor so without a moment to lose, I guzzled it up too. Now that's what I can a real two for one!

With a belly as big as a full moon, I waddled out to the garden with Rob, who had his mug of tea in hand. This was my supervised play time and my minder, or playground assistant, was on hand to sort out any trouble I may find myself in for the ten minutes I was afforded to run off some steam before he needed to go and get ready for work. As I was so like a giant space hopper about to topple over, I just sat for a time observing Coco and Bubby chasing a minging green slavery tennis ball that was kicked for them by Rob. Once my digestive juices had gotten to work and I had passed some wind to reduce my swelly belly, I tried to join in with the ugly sisters but they weren't for playing ball with me. Selfish so they were! I hadn't seen their mug shots in any of the newspapers I'd come across or they would have drowned by now and I would be the only dog in existence.

a lab report

With our allotted time over, Bubby and Coco retreated to their plush beds in the study and I was transported back upstairs to my generational bed and Rob shut the door firmly behind him as he exited. This afforded him peace and quiet to have breakfast, shower and dress without me trying to steal his socks or chew his shoes.

As Rob left the house he shouted up, "See you later, love you all."

Amy responded, "Love you too," and then the door clicked shut behind him.

It was puppy attention time. I hopped out of my bed and whizzed up to beside Amy; one arm was dangling out from beneath the covers. I nuzzled at it and got no reaction so licked it ferociously causing her to retract it back under the covers quick smart. She tilted her head to look at me and then reached down towards me and scooped me up on to the bed sheets. I scanned for George the monkey but no visible sign of him. Shame! Amy cuddled me towards her and kissed my cheek and then curled herself back in to a wee ball and placed me, on top of the covers, beside her tummy.

"Just fifteen minutes more snoozing time then we'll get up," she mumbled in a sleepy tone.

I snuggled in and played dead for about the whole of two minutes. At that point I couldn't contain myself any longer and unannounced, darted up the covers and sprang on her head and started chewing her hair. My bald belly engulfed her face and my paws slid from side to side all over her ears and neck as I tried to brace myself for a good chomp (I liked chomps too if there were no dentastixs available). I tugged and pulled at her hair and she squealed with delight. She was now fully awake and was playing with me by tossing her head from side to side so I could get bigger chunks of brown locks in my mouth. This was fun. A few seconds later Amy, obviously less than impressed by my exploits, grabbed hold of my scruff and peeled me from her face. She held me high in the air.

"You wee monster," she said. "So much for a long lie. I may as well just get up!"

She placed me down on to the floor, flung the duvet back splattering me in all her bed mites, slipped on her bathrobe and headed to the mirror to admire herself. Her hair had that lovely bed-head look and I had done an excellent job at back combing it; she looked very becoming and I knew that Vital Seeyasoon would have been equally impressed. She had some fierce lines across her face that seemed to make her look like a native Red Indian. Either that or she had aged overnight and would need to go for some botox injections to restore her youthful appearance. There was extreme pressure on her to look attractive; that expectation came with ownership of me. Coming from a long line of show champions I am blessed with stunning good looks, great intellect and even a black beauty spot on my tongue. Sadly gundogs were not really born with any of the aforementioned and Coco, poor soul, although relatively good looking for a gundog, paled in to insignificance alongside me. Bubby, who was now ninety four, only had a little grey hair around her muzzle and was a bit deaf at times; like my human granny. I certainly didn't need to worry about any competition from

a lab report

that pair! What a fine specimen I am. Have I already said that?

Having washed and eaten Amy took us all out for a walk through the local estate. Saying a walk is perhaps exaggerating a bit as mine consisted of being stuck in a small ruck sack worn on her front like some hemmed-in baby. Although I was able to peek out it was boring as nowt and I made my break for freedom when she bent down to scoop up some poop, which she gathered up using her hand placed in some green bag – yuck! (I loved how humans were our slaves). She tied the poo bag tightly and then hung it decoratively from a loop on her rucksack - Berghaus thought of everything! On cold days, she sometimes put the warm poopie bag in her pocket and used it as a hand warmer. Even bigger yuck! As she did all of this I knew her eyes were firmly fixed on me and my escape from Ruckatraz would be short lived so I made the most of my time by sniffing out a dead field mouse and doing my dying-fly impression on top of it. Luckily for Amy, monsieur mouse was well past its sell by date and so dried up nothing stuck to my coat. As my nose is super sensitive I could smell the eau du parfum left on my fur coat and for this reason was pleased with my short field trip. After being grabbed by the tail, secured in Amy's hands, I was ticked off and then tucked back in the ruck sack. The zip was pulled up high to stop me escaping again, and almost choking me to death, we continued our walk.

At the end of the fields was an algae monster infested swamp and I saw Coco plunge in to it and emerge from it with a green, gangrenous coat and brandishing a stick she had swum to pick up. She then ran off in to the woods to go 'squizzy bashing' which meant chasing the squirrels up the trees. Coco would try to climb up the tree after them and it was amusing watching the squirrels taunt her from the upper branches as they leapt from one to the other well out of her reach. This just reinforced my belief that beyond the basic retrieving commands that were genetic in gundogs, they were not the sharpest tacks in the box, as I would have called it quits at this point and moved on to my next target! Bubby never had any intention of exerting herself chasing anything but her dementiated state caused her to put on the odd spurt for no reason I could figure out. Now and then Amy would coax her with a treat dangled from her hand in order to speed her up when we were running tight for time; which happened to be today as Amy and I were off out visiting one of Amy's friends, called the vet, in a short time.

    Once back home it was a quick turnaround. Amy hooked up Coco, on her lead, to the banister in the garden while she got the hose ready to blast her coat with an icy shower of water to ensure she no longer looked like the Incredible Hulk. As soon as the hose was started up Coco thrashed her head back and fore, slipped her collar and scurried behind one of the bushes in the garden. As Amy moved towards her to grab her and haul her back to the shower, she put on this ferocious looking face, barked and bolted off across to the far side of the garden. This was proving great entertainment for me and Bubby, who cheered her on by barking as loud as we could from the side-lines. Eventually Amy used Coco's lead to lasso her and pull her back to base for her hosing; which I am sure lasted much longer than it would have if she had played ball in the first instance! After a quick towel dry Coco and Bubby were put back

a lab report

in the house and given a dentastix each to keep their gnashers in fine form. I was bundled up inside Amy's fleecy and given no such treat. I presumed I must be getting something at her friend's.

"See you in a while girls. We're away off to the vet to get Rosie's first jag."

Wow I thought: Am I getting my own car? Was I not too young to get my licence and drive such an expensive, powerful machine? Maybe they hadn't forgotten my birthday present after all. I glanced down quickly and saw Coco and Bubby looking up at me, adoringly, with grins on them like a pair of Cheshire Cats. It was the first time since my arrival that both of them had looked so happy for me and showed me any real sign of acceptance. I was intrigued that they did not seem upset or jealous in any way that I was getting taken out somewhere special by myself or by the no expense spared approach to my first birthday present. What nice dogs after all I thought to myself.

Once we'd locked the door behind us we headed to Rob's car (he used Amy's for commuting during the week and kindly left Amy his estate car for transporting us dogs around). She opened the boot and popped me in. After she pressed a button it closed automatically behind her and I was cordoned off in this smallish area. This was the first time I had been in the car since I'd been brought here, when I had been cuddled closely against Amy in her cosy top. It was kind of scary here in the back by myself. There was a set of bars, somewhat like a prison, separating me from me the passenger and driver areas. Given that I was so tiny at the moment there was no way I could manage to climb up to look

47

through these never mind escape anywhere. As she drove along the coastal road, with its many bends, I was turfed from side to side, like a snooker ball being played off the side cushions of the table; at least it ended up in a pocket at some point! I, however, had to endure about ten minutes of this fate before arriving at the veterinary surgery. Lucky for Amy, I didn't throw up en route but even if I had, as most dogs do, I would have re-consumed the evidence by the time of arrival. I know some of you may baulk in disgust, but we all know that most of us appreciate things more second time around. They always have a deeper flavour.

When the boot opened I sat in the furthest corner from her reach, still stunned from my journey. There were no visible signs for her to acknowledge my turbulent time so as I moved towards her I did my best impression of a drunk person. I think she got the message as she looked pityingly at me,

"Oh, sweet pea. Are you a bit shell-shocked from your journey here? I am so used to Coco and Bubby being much bigger that I totally forgot that you'd get flung around a little in the back. I'll get a vented box from the vets for you to travel back in."

I was then plucked from the boot and carried in to the vets surgery. Once through the door, my celebrity status was obvious as the vet nurses, and other customers, were like bees around a honey pot. There were hands patting my head, my body, my whiskers and any other part that could be reached. There were voices saying, 'So how old are you?' and, 'Is she a pure Lab?' I managed to fire a filthy look in the direction of the lady that asked that. She mustn't know a good thing when she sees it and that was evident as later, when I sat

a lab report

down to wait my turn, I noticed she had a cat.

As we were sitting in the waiting room a lady in a blue coat came over to speak to me. Amy announced,

"Rosie, meet Rosie."

What? Someone had the same name as me! Apparently I had been named after one of the vet nurses who had treated Coco when she was very ill and nursed her back to health following her ordeal. Coco had a run in with some ant powder which my human granny had put on the paving in her garden to kill off the ants but Coco had ended up lying in it and it nearly got rid of her instead. She had got a caustic burn and had to have her coat shaved off in different parts of her body (ears, sides and tail. She must have looked hilariously ridiculous with her alopecia). She was homed at the vets' surgery for nearly a week as they cared for her 24/7. Rosie had bathed her, swathed her in cream, fed her and her tender loving care cured her. What a champion she had been and had done such a brilliant job Amy and Rob got Coco back alive and kicking. I was so proud to have been named after such a Good Samaritan. I had a lot to live up to.

As I sat with Amy awaiting my appointment to see her friend the vet, I tired myself out my running round and round her head and over her shoulders. This seemed to amuse the other people waiting so I continued to show off until I got a little dizzy and had to stop. I then moved on to chomping her fingers and fleecy jacket. Noticing my boredom had reached new heights Amy wandered over to the area with toys and treats in it. She took the odd toy off the pegs they were hanging on and let me smell them. I didn't like the latex type ones; they smelt funny and I'd be able to destroy them in a matter of seconds. I took a fancy for one that looked quite like Snoopy. He was about my size and had a brown circle round one of his eyes. He also had black ears and was quite handsome for a fake. I managed to get one of his ears in my slavery mouth when Amy brought him down to show me so she ended up having to buy him for me as a 'positive reinforcement' for my first visit here. Aptly enough, I named him 'Patch'. There was a Patch in my village as well, but he wasn't as handsome as my new dog. I was eight weeks old and had my own dog that was as big as me, cost nothing to feed and whom I didn't have to walk and who could play with me and never win. Just my type of friend.

"Rosie"

I looked up to see Rosie calling my name; or was it her own name and she was looking for early retirement on the grounds of diminished responsibility or madness? I was so glad my coat was black, as Rosie's blue one wasn't a flattering colour for people called by our name.

"This way, please."

I was carried through to a minute room off the main corridor. There was a lady in a white coat in the room. What's with the different colours of coats I thought? I didn't like white either and wondered if she was called Rosie too.

"So who have we got here then?"

"I am Rosie," I said holding out my paw to introduce myself.

"I am 8 weeks old today and I come from a hilltop house in the Trossachs. I have twelve brothers and sisters and my Mum was

a lab report

a golden lab and my Dad a black one. And who are you?"

As if Amy could read my mind, she told my story, the way I just have, almost verbatim. The vet I was seeing today was called Lucy. She had a warming pitch to her voice and looked at me adoringly; I liked her but wondered what she was doing touching me all over on a high black table. She then turned round to her computer and filled in some information on me on her screen. One short sentence would sum me up 'Drop dead gorgeous Lab called Rosie.'

She then turned round to look at me and explained to Amy that as part of my first health check she would need to weigh me, check my temperature and my teeth. Once she'd done that she would get on and give me my first inoculation. I guess she would also want to take some paw prints too as I knew they did when humans went through passport control. Then she may ask me to give her a swab with my saliva on it for DNA purposes should I commit any crimes in the future. That would be easy I thought; if she visited me at a meal time she could catch some slavers on her cotton bud as they foamed at the side of my mouth or bathe them in the pool left behind on the tiles. Her choice.

Rosie was then asked to weigh me and took me back through to the main surgery, with my little red lead on and placed me on this humungous treadmill looking object and shouted, "Run" (only joking). She set the scales to zero and then did her best to get me to play statues, like I have to at feeding times when asked to sit, so she could get a reading. Eighty stone it said. I wondered if my human granny had arrived and stood on the scales at the back of me. I glanced round quickly to check - nope, no sign of! "Eight pounds," Rosie said aloud. So there I was, eight weeks old and weighing in at eight zero pounds. Did I have eight teeth as well? I was now standing on the black table again and was getting this funny thing stuck up my bottom, which was a tad uncomfortable. I wriggled about a little and clenched my buttocks. It was held in there by Lucy for a few seconds and then extracted. Luckily it came out minus any of my stinky stuff, even though I did a little pump at the same time as it was being removed. I smiled with glee and not embarrassment. The familiar smell of my earlier food ruminating around the treatment room felt comforting in this strange place where I was being poked and prodded. After a quick flicking of the thermometer Lucy reported that I was 'normal'. What a cheek to make such a flippant, throw away comment. I was far from normal. I was superhuman or should I say 'wonder dog'. It took me a moment or two to realise she was referring to my body temperature.

After taking hold of my chin in one hand and top lip in her other, Lucy prised my mouth open and had a look inside my small cavern of stalagmites and stalactites.

"Hmm......" she sounded concerned.

"It is early days but it looks as though Rosie has two pre-molar teeth missing – one on her upper set and the other on her lower set. We will just a keep a wee eye on this and see if there is any sign of these coming in when she comes back for her second inoculation in 4 weeks' time."

Lucy turned to the white bench behind her and lifted up a

a lab report

syringe with a big sharp needle pointing out of it. After inserting it in to a small jar and filling it up with liquid, she swiftly took hold of my scruff and plunged the sharp point in to the skin beneath my coat. On removing the offending obstacle she massaged the area she had just pierced it in to. Luckily for me I hadn't felt a thing.

"While you're here, we'll just do her identity chip too. We wouldn't want such a precious soul going undetected if she ever went missing, would we?"

I guessed that was a rhetorical question. So there I was, a second jag, with what looked like a grain of rice being fired in to me. I wondered if Amy got a PIN number for me too?

"What a good girl you are. That's Rosie finished for today. Except for the teeth which we'll keep an eye on, you've got a beautiful, healthy puppy there."

I repeated the sentence over and over in my head, lingering on the 'beautiful' part. I was destined for great things and beauty pageants across the world. I had decided I wouldn't do too many in order to give other dogs a chance, but it was important to at least strut my stuff a few times to a make a statement and share my glamour with the wider world.

We paid at the desk on the way out and Amy took the liberty of purchasing a small cardboard box for my journey home. When we got to the car she squeezed the box in to the foot-well of the passenger seat, opened up the lid and placed me inside. She put Patch in with me and then closed the top over. It was dark but as Patch was white he helped light up the box and acted as a soft bouncer when we hit the bends of the coast road. As we journeyed home I managed to chew off a bit of Patch's ear and eat it; Amy would see the evidence of this in approximately twenty-four hours when she picked up my poopie in the garden (My number twos would prove a great source of information for many of my misgivings in the future and sometimes as a source of reclaiming items - you will be amazed what I have managed to digest in my year and a half of life. I am the canine version of 'Lost and Found').

In my final few minutes of being homeward bound I managed to create a larger ventilation hole in the cardboard, and as Amy pulled in to the drive, she noticed one of my legs was now protruding and waving frantically out one of the sides of the box. Had I been given more time, me and Patch would have found our way out and have been running free. Even being two teeth short didn't seem to affect my Harry Houdini exploits and, if they ever did a canine version of the Shawshank Redemption, I would be best placed to take the lead part.

a lab report

5

Eight to Twelve Weeks - The Learning Stage

The next four weeks were fairly similar to the first few days at Residence de Bubby, Coco and Rosie. I'd spend my nights sleeping with Patch, who tended to take up much more of my bed than I had envisaged but served as a source of amusement to me in the wee, small hours of darkness. With my persistent handy work and remodelling of his body parts, in particular his ears, he now bore a striking resemblance to Vincent Van Gogh but was certainly no oil painting next to me.

I continued to be fed three times daily but spent longest over my lunch-time meal, which was the one Bubby and Coco didn't get. It would be uncharitable to suggest that my prolonged consumption of this meal was purely as a measure to tease them. I merely slowed things down as it aided my digestion - the slower I ate the less my tummy ballooned meaning I didn't look like I had just swallowed a water melon. Sometimes after eating Rob would try to make a fool of me and my bulbous belly by moving his hand above my head in a circular motion and then over it towards the back of it. As he did so I would follow him with my eyes and before I knew it, I would have fallen backwards on to the floor like some drunk man. As I was such a roly-poly I was unable to stop myself and he would laugh mockingly at me, referring to me as 'Tubby, Tub.' Not funny. I would be phoning Dogline if this continued, to report a serious case of bullying. In the meantime I would just have to deal with it my own way as targeted children often did. I clambered back up on to my paws and attempted to maul his feet as pay back for humiliating me. He had better watch out I thought, being one of thirteen pups had taught me how to plan revenge and I would be the one to have the last laugh as he would find out later when I chewed up his expensive Calvin Kling boxers.

During the day, every day, and in between my all-important meals, Amy tried her best to train me and instil some discipline in to my life. I would have my red, chewed, tufty collar clipped around my neck and a long red lead would be attached to its D ring. It may have been a matching set but given they were 'hand me downs' and not specifically purchased for me, there would be no way I was going to perform to my best. One could never be expected to in substandard clothing or equipment!

Fully clad I would be marched round the garden with

a lab report

commands such as 'heel', 'sit' and 'walk on' said authoritatively to me. I took 'heel' as instructing me to try to prise Amy's shoes off her feet as I did with her slippers. I had mastered that skill soon after arrival and was a gold starred pupil at that. Why she tapped her leg at the same time as giving the 'heel' command confused me as I couldn't see any foot or shoe up there. Once we were speeding along I would do my best to burl round and round, so I would end up choking on the lead and she'd have to stop to untangle me. Alternatively I would try to chomp my way through it by jumping up and down at it, getting my teeth stuck in it, and end up being pulled along, spinning around and being dragged along on my back like some rag doll. Amy took little notice of my attempts to obstruct her training so I would step up a gear at this point. I'd self-select the 'sit' command and no amount of encouragement from her would move me one iota. Well, perhaps one of these smelly fish treats she kept in her pocket would entice me to venture a few steps further before sitting down again. Eventually, fed up from my shenanigans, Amy would unhook my lead and unclip my reprobate's collar and leave me outside to play with my sisters. I could tell she was getting fed up with my behaviour but after all, I was a mere puppy and unless I behaved like one she would be disappointed - wouldn't she?

Left unattended in the garden I found lots of new and exciting things to do. I raced through the daffodils and rolled around in them until they were as flat as pancakes. I'd then help Amy with her flower arranging by yanking some heads off the lilies, tulips and the squashed daffies, and sprinkle them around the garden so she could see my hard work and talents in flower re-arranging. If she was clever she could gather them up later and make a Posie for Rosie from them. I would probably be laying low when she did this as I am sure all would not be Rosie in the garden as she cursed under her breath about her ever depleting blooms!

Further to this I set to task digging up some bulbs in the rockery and eating some of the hard, decorative white pellet things in-between the heathers and lavender bushes; I believe these were called stones. They certainly lacked taste but they made my belly feel full and heavy after I had about three of them; they also made me sound like a rattle-snake for as I ran around, they jiggled about inside me.

When I saw Coco coming to check out what I was up to I'd run straight in to the Leylandia and weave in and out of it so she couldn't catch me. Problem was when I finally did appear back out the hedge she would inevitably molicate me for trying to be smart.

Sometimes during more peaceful times I would join Bubby eating the green grass in the pasture of the back garden. However I would spice things up by mixing my weed and eating some of the yellowy coloured stuff as well which seemed to have more of an acidic taste. Bubby used to look bemused as I munched my way through it and no wonder as I later discovered, in my infinite wisdom, now that I am an older dog, that I was eating dead grass as a result of urine poisoning by my sisters. It was at this point I understood why dogs regularly chucked up after eating it!

The kennels in the garden were a point of intrigue to me. The handmade one, which could fit all three of us, was impressive

a lab report

with its slatted wood exterior and centrally heated interior with fancy radiators which were thermostatically controlled from the outside (to sleep per chance to dream). The entrance step was so ginormous that Amy had put a little pallet of wood down for me to enable me to gain access to my palace. The opening arch was large enough that I could climb in without stooping at all. The straw covering the floor smelt of Coco's sweaty feet and made me feel a tad nauseous. I popped my head out for some fresh air for a few seconds and took a huge gasp in, filled my lungs up and then holding my breath, continued my quick inspection of the kennel. It was quite swanky and had a panoramic view of the garden from the back window. With the odd little bit of re-arranging by me it would be perfect and serve as picnic spot for me to munch on my pinched fruit or vegetables from the garden or, alternatively, as a place to stash my stolen goods.

    I took a jump out the kennel, missing the pallet completely and careering headlong into the single dog's kennel opposite. I was met with a fierce growl and Bubby stood up, thumped passed me and flung me to the ground in one fell swoop. Superb I thought as I picked myself up and dusted my paws off. At least now it was vacant so I could venture in and look around uninterrupted to see if this kennel was of a standard suitable for a prime pooch like me. Quite cramped, I thought, and no window like in the mansion next door. Obviously the rental would be lower, but as I was from a wealthy background money was no object, so I would certainly be cohabiting in the upper market kennel with Coco. This smaller kennel was most certainly designed for cross-breeds who didn't have the same standards as us pedigrees. I spun round quickly and exited to the fresh air. I took a deep breath, drew in some clean air to my lungs and then headed back indoors through the flap, which was a cinch now that I knew to head-butt it first before flinging the rest of my body through!

Indoors was my second play area. There was a multitude of things to get up to. In the hallway, opposite the dog flap, was the downstairs shower room. More often than not, Amy and Rob would forget to pull the door closed behind them and there would be a more than ample gap for me to nose it open and make my way to that elusive toilet roll that was so closely guarded. I had got hold of the toilet roll on about day two of me being here and chomped my way through a good bit of it and the rest ended up around my teeth and inside of my cheeks, making me look like a squirrel storing nuts for the winter. Amy had to spend a considerable amount of time scraping it out my mouth and then picking up the remnants of what I had swallowed in my poopie over the following days; processing time could be slow in puppies which was extremely annoying for humans especially if they were deliberating over whether you had stolen something of theirs or not.

I nudged the door open and bounced three or four steps towards the toilet holder. Some days I was in luck and they had forgotten to remove it from its holder and place it in the under sink cabinet. Within seconds I managed to use my front paws to climb up the bit of wall beside the loo roll and use my pincers to wrench it off and down on to the tiles. If it was a fresh roll it was too big for my mouth, so instead of carrying it around I needed to

a lab report

revert to finding an end piece. I would then grip on to this bit, run out the bathroom, through the dining room, up the hall stairs, with it unfurling behind me - leaving my own paper trail and a clue to where I might be found - not very clever in terms of hiding my evidence.

The first time Rob saw me perform this trick he yelled on Amy in excitement proclaiming,

"We have a real Andrex puppy!"

Given that it was a source of such amusement and almost condoned by Rob (well, his enthusiasm was deemed to be encouragement in my eyes) I took every opportunity I could to repeat it.

In my early days I had a fetish for all things white, be it socks, bras, knickers or Rob's boxers, and for a real tasty treat, tissues – preferably of the used variety. Thank goodness Amy hadn't had a baby yet or I am sure nappies would have also featured; I had never tasted second-hand baby food but I had a spirit of adventure and was always game to try new things.

I also acquired a liking for Amy's wool jumpers, shoes, tights and slippers. I was born a kleptomaniac and would pinch whatever was available to me and use my inner talents to create designer patterns in both the clothing and shoes. I remember finding a really special pair of patent leather shoes in Amy's dressing room; they had a lovely shine to them and I liked moving around in front of them and seeing my reflection change as if I was in a hall of mirrors. I looked stunning in all my shapes and forms. After loving the bones of myself, I picked up one of the pretty shoes and hid under the bed and spent some minutes re-modelling it in to something I deemed even more fashionable. I have impeccably good taste and an eye for detail and was keen to demonstrate my creative talents to the full. When finished, and unable to give the same due care and attention to the matching shoe, not that it matched at the moment, I left it stored discreetly for another date and time when I could fetch the other one and compare and contrast them together to complete the job. I was meticulous in terms of always seeing projects through from inception to completion; no half measures for me. However, I was not afforded this opportunity as later on that day, Amy found my masterpiece under the bed. To say she was apoplectic with rage would be an understatement. Apparently she had bought these beautiful, one-off, designer stilettos in some posh boutique in Hong Kong only the previous summer when en route to Australia to visit her sister. She was at pains to point out to me, as she frantically waved the shoe in the air, that they could not be replaced. How selfish I thought given I had spent so much quality time making them unique. I could have blamed my best friend, Vinnie Van Patch but I am not sure I would have been believed! I was also proud of my workdogship, so why would I have wanted to pass the buck anyway?

During these weeks I also discovered my tail. I would turn round and see this black thing following me so, every now and again, I would pounce on it with the aim of catching it in my mouth. Holding tightly on to it, I'd spin round and round like on a merry-go-round, holding on to the tip of it as tightly as possible, even though it was always fighting to get away from

a lab report

me. Eventually, exhausted and feeling giddy, I'd land in a heap on the floor with my tail having made its escape. After a few seconds of coming too I'd stumble back on to my feet and start all over again. I would not be beaten.

Scrounging became a new pastime. In the evening, around seven, Amy and Rob would eat dinner. Given I had gorged my face an hour previous, my belly had shrunk enough to be able to squeeze in some more. Almost as soon as they sat down Bubby would wander into the dining room and demand to be let through to the rear hallway so she could exit to the back garden to bark herself silly; a ritual she would repeat every night of her existence. I took to joining her as I liked to watch her pretend to be fierce at nothingness; if you ask me it was the early signs of dementia. Given my developing grey matter she was going to pose little challenge to me, the Adonis and Einstein of the canine variety.

After a few minutes Amy would get fed up and bang on the French doors, gesturing for her to come back in before she got complaints from the surrounding neighbours. After doing a few extra ferocious barks, as she always had to have the last word, she would head back indoors making her presence known. She would fling the door wide open causing it to bang forcefully off the wall and letting the cold air sweep in. I would totter in behind her and slink under the table, pretending I was invisible thus increasing my opportunity to catch any dropped food. Bubby would lie on the tiles beside Rob's feet. Coco would remain outside the dining room, on the carpet, with eyes firmly focused on Amy, scrutinising her every mouthful. The instant Amy finished Coco, who was scared of all types of flooring and avoided puddles in case she got her feet wet, (weird for a gundog) would cautiously push past the door and treading carefully on the tiles, make her way to her side to scrounge what was left on her plate. Coco would then perform her Niagara Falls act, leaving slavers all over the side of Amy's leather chair, forcing her to use her napkin to catch her dangling drools and wipe up the mucus pool on the floor. Having observed all of this I had now renamed Coco - Sloberdan Cocovich.

I then turned my attention to watching Bubby, who was very much the lady of the household and never a slaver should pass from her mouth. She didn't have floppies like me and Coco and was very tight lipped. She was a femme fatale and I believed she thought she was derived from gentry; she had this peculiar way of looking down her big, long, pointed Doberman nose at us mere mortals or pure breeds. Labradors were more common than cross breeds she had commented to me once - every second person has a black Lab especially in the village we lived in. Sometimes there were so many of us together in the local fields that our owners could barely identify us and it took calling our names repeatedly to get us to report in and even then they'd check over our name tags. Most of the time I would just ignore Amy or Rob, when they called me, especially when I was in hot pursuit of one of the more wimpy Labs and about to send them in to a sausage roll and stampede over them. Sometimes frustration of waiting for me to come back would kick in and as I tanked past, Rob would try to dive rugby tackle me; this was hilarious and I got a great kick out of watching him dirty his trousers and jacket as he fell to the ground, missing capturing

a lab report

me by miles. Finally, as I began to get tired I would allow myself to be caught by my collar and my rope training-lead would be slipped over my head. Amazingly, even for my naughty, childish behaviour, I would still be rewarded with a 'good girl' and a minute treat. My owners knew from training previous dogs never to say 'bad dog' or give a row for not coming back or taking my time to return to them as this just caused resentment and ended up with the dog playing up for ages as they were too frightened to come back. A treat and an eventual return was better than none at all.

Bubby stood out for being an individual and certainly looked, to put it politely, different. There may have been an iota of truth in what she said about us being one a penny although I would never admit it. However I was so dazzlingly and glamorous I was always identifiable in any clan gathering.

Reverting back to my scranning - I do tend to veer off at tangents but this is to be expected in a developing brain. The morsels left on Amy and Rob's plates were always divided in to three pieces; two big bits and a bite sized bit for little young me. As I watched the process of dividing by a third (I was good at fractions) bubbles inflated and deflated at the side of my mouth, proportionately increasing in numbers relative to the time I waited for my tit bits. Actually, to help you picture the speed at which they mass produced it was strikingly similar to the numbers of those created by pouring bubble bath under a hot tap. Get the picture? I now looked like I had an extreme dose of rabies as I foamed at the mouth in anticipation. As Amy reached down towards me I snatched the food from her fingers and swallowed it over at pace. My morsels seemed to have little or no taste but perhaps the speed at which I guzzled it down may have contributed to this. Mind you, I would argue that what I was given was so insignificant in size it was barely worth getting excited over.

Once we had all finished our nosh Rob would hold up his cracked pads, and say, "All gone" and cross his hands back and fore over each other like he was a magician who had caused something to vanish. I know he was referring to the food all having gone but it was a pity he couldn't make the terrible two disappear. Alas he wasn't that talented!

Bubby and Coco exited to the living room to chill, loll across the leather sofa and snore so loudly that it sounded like a storm was in full swing. I would linger for a moment or two longer; sometimes this would work in my favour as Amy seemed to be able to draw together some more scraps from her plate and press them together in to a special treat just for me. Scrumptious.

a lab report

6

Twelve Weeks Old

I arrived at the vet in all my splendour. This time I travelled in the boot and as I was a little bigger in size, managed to keep my footing for most of the journey. I had not been placed in the travel box Amy had purchased previously as Patch and I had found it so claustrophobic and dark we agreed then that we would not succumb to such poor standards of transport in the future, so we had completely trashed it on our return home by performing Kung Fu Patch moves on it. My old faithful friend, Patch, sat beside me and was accompanying me on this, my second visit to the vet and, to be honest, by the look of him, was in more need of surgery than I was.

When we pulled up at the surgery, Amy opened the boot

and grabbed hold of my scruff in super-quick time before I had the opportunity to make any attempt to jump out and run off. Unlike the first time, when I was tiny tottie and Amy had carried me in securely tucked under her arm, now I was a bit bigger, Amy had to put in some more extreme precautionary measures to ensure she had a super glue grip of me. To be frank, I really didn't feel like doing a runner at this moment in time as my memories of my first visit were not too harrowing, except perhaps for the cold thermometer up the bottom. I had liked the aroma it had caused afterwards so every cloud could have a silver lining after all. The fact that Patch had been visiting on the same day as me and come home with us afterwards had also been a huge bonus. We were best buddies now.

Amy reached in to her pocket and brought out a flashy new collar which she clipped around my rotund neck. It was multi-coloured and brought out the colour of my eyes; well the red did. I was then tucked under her arm and she hooked a few fingers under my posh collar so she could hold on tightly to me should I attempt to wriggle free in the waiting area to molest a few cats should there be any. Hopefully that ignorant cat woman wouldn't be there this time; I never forget people who cross me and I could still picture her screwed up little face asking if I was a real Labrador. Hmm!

I had remembered that my namesake worked here and expected Rosie would be around to roll out the red carpet for me and welcome me like a celebrity.

Once in the surgery I was again surrounded by little people, known as kids, wanting to clap me and the veterinary nurses also to shower me in compliments. Oh what it's like to be me.......! Is

a lab report

that not a song? I scoured the waiting area to see who there was available to sit next too. A cat would be good as I could give it the evil eye and make it considerably more uncomfortable than it was already while awaiting its appointment. Amy would be unable to see my lip curling from above and me baring my vicious milk teeth at it (well the ones I had). I finally woke up to my senses with the calling of my name. It was my turn to go through to the parlour and be a pampered pooch. Bubby and Coco had told me that they came here for manicures and pedicures. I believed that that was the posh way of saying they came to get their nails clipped. Not quite so appealing when put like that!

I was now seated on the table in the vets consulting room and Lucy, the same vet as I saw last time, was smiling at me with her face close in to mine and she looked like some big giant about to eat me. She was rubbing my ears with her hands, and every now and then would cradle my face and tilt it from side to side.

"Well you have grown a little since I saw you last, honey pie," she said to me.

I had never tasted honey pie myself but I imagined it to be sweet and scrummy like me. She then asked Amy how I had been since the last time I had been there. I awaited Amy's response, wondering if she would tell her the truth about all my adventures. However she told Lucy that I was eating well, loved to play and be busy in the garden and that I got on well with Bubby and Coco. Lucy asked if I was house trained yet. I looked at her in disbelief. I had been house trained within forty eight hours of being at my new home and was clever enough to have even worked out the dog flap. I was amazing! Lucy explained to me and Amy that today was a case of a quick health check again and then giving me the second part of my booster so I could go out and about and be fully protected.

To start the health check Lucy ran her hands over my head, along my spine, over my body and down my back legs. I wasn't used to strangers feeling me up and my body tensed a little as she did so. With the usual tension came the eruption of a humongous fart as my body reacted to the stress. Eau de Rosie Posie. Amy looked at me and giggled a little; out of embarrassment I am sure. I stuck my nose high in the air and breathed deeply, filling my lungs with the sweet heaven scent. Mmmmmmm... After a quick look in my cavern and the identification of the 'still' non-appearance of a pre-molar on the lower right and a molar on the upper left, I was discharged with Rosie, my alter-ego vet nurse, for a weigh-in through in the back room. I bet I was still in the featherweight category! I was placed in a dish this time, hooked up to a weighing scale, and clocked in at twelve pounds. Super heavy weight compared to my previous eight pounds. When I returned to the surgery, I cottoned on to the fact that things smelt a little fresher and I noticed on the back desk, beside the computer that logged all my details, the small, insignificant can of air-fresher that had been sprayed round the surgery in my absence. It was a much inferior quality of perfume than mine and I would imagine that it had been purchased in some bargain basement. I showed my displeasure by sneezing a few times on re-entry. These things caused allergies! Back on the table, and held tightly by Amy, I had a rather

a lab report

large looking syringe pushed in to the back of my scruff, liquid squirted in to me and then the needle taken out and my neckline rubbed with the tips of Lucy's fingers.

"That's you pup. Good to go."

"Good to go where?" I thought. The vet told Amy to give the jag two days to work and then I could go out for walks anywhere. My mind spun out of control at the prospect of seeing other places outwith the sanctity of my own garden or Amy and Rob's jackets. I was about to run, play and hunt with the big dogs and show them who was boss.

j s carle

7

My First Real Walk

It was now the middle of June and I was about to go out for my first ever walk beyond my garden. I was appropriately dressed in my new collar which had my name tag and contact details on it just in case I ran off and got lost. Obviously Rob and Amy would not want to lose such a precious being as myself even though I had been microchipped as back up.

Rob headed out first with Coco and Bubby on the 'big walk' as at my mere age I was unable to withstand the distance that pair could with my developing limbs. I had heard Amy arranging to meet him at the flagpole, which was near the end of the bay, and adjacent to a small beach. Here Amy and I could sit and wait for

a lab report

Rob and the gruesome twosome and I could play off my lead in 'relative safety' (whatever that meant).

We headed out about fifteen minutes after the reprobates had left and I was linked up to my lead at the end of the path before we passed through the garden gate. I sat ever so prettily to have my lead attached to my new, yes I said new, collar, to give the notion that I was going to behave on this first adventure in to pastures new. I was fairly adept at walking on my lead now as I had put in four weeks of practising walking around the garden on it. The first two weeks I had wrestled with it but Amy or it didn't seem to want to play ball. With a little tenacity over the two successive weeks I successfully chewed massive chunks out of it, forcing Amy to invest in a heavier, more durable lead made of toughened rope - like the ones you get for mooring boats which are basically indestructible! I think she was trying to convey a strong message to me.

Once out the gate we walked to the end of the drive and Amy, in her school teacher's voice, instructed me in to 'sit' at the same time as pushing my booty to the ground. What fun this walk is going to be I thought. Seconds later we were off on a trot up the Main Street. There were these funny big metal things on wheels passing by me on the road. They towered over me and were quite frightening so I just kept looking straight ahead trying to pretend they weren't there. I had heard Brambles became scared when a bus or lorry was thundering through the village and she would reportedly run and jump behind a wall and hide out until it had vanished out of sight. Her behaviour was curiouser and curiouser and portrayed Labermans (my term for a Labrador/Doberman cross) as real cowards. This proved she was not quite the tough dog she liked me to think she was and now I knew she had weaknesses there was a chink in her chain to exploit at a later stage, should I ever need to do so.

As I continued my walk along the street I took sufficient time to sniff every piece of litter, bit of food or mark on the pavement that I came across and tried to lick up the odd bit that seemed to be chocolate. I read somewhere that chocolate was highly poisonous for dogs and should not be consumed under any circumstances; unless, like me, you come across a minuscule bit on your walk that you can lick up and savour, as that opportunity is like finding gold dust.

Once on to the main Bay Road I met some children who were drawn to me like I was candy floss. They picked me up and cuddled me and I licked their ears and faces. Not very hygienic I know as you never know where they have been! Hopefully now I was fully inoculated I would not catch anything from them. Further down nearer the bay we met some big dogs; an Irish Wolfhound and a Labrador/Spaniel (Spaniels are mad as brushes) cross called Marty. He was quite cute, mainly because he took a distinct shine to moi. I couldn't help admire a dog with good taste, even if he was another cross-breed. After he had sniffed me all over, and I mean all over as I had lain on my back and bared my all to the world, we continued on to the beachy bit.

Amazingly, Rob, Coco and Bubby were already there; they must have walked their section exceptionally fast knowing that they would be meeting me. Amy dropped my lead and allowed me

a lab report

to run the few metres in front of her to meet Rob. He clapped his hands together repeatedly at the same time as calling my name. I ran straight towards him at speed, and at the very last minute, did a body swerve past him and headed straight for Coco for a game of chasey. Bubby also joined in and we played-piggy-in-the-middle, or should that be puppy-in-the-middle, as I seemed to get bowled over by both of them for the next few minutes until Amy produced a treat from her pocket and waved it in the air. At this point food-focused greedy Coco darted over to her, followed in hot pursuit by Bubby and then me. We all got 'Good girls' said to us along with a treat for coming. As I was given my treat my lead was attached firmly to my collar. We spent a further ten minutes or so at the beach, where Coco and Bubby had a stick thrown for them to retrieve from the sea. Coco powered out using her webbed feet to propel her through the water at speed and snatch the stick from the ocean's surface. She'd then swim it back to shore for the monstrous Bubby to seize it out if her mouth as she made land. Bubby knew exactly how to have a dog and not bark herself and regularly used unassuming Coco to do her donkey (or should I say 'dog') work for her. Coco was not a total push over however and she would do her best to try and steal it back but Bubby was obviously top dog and after a few attempts, Coco would retract and bounce off in to the water to await a new stick being thrown by Amy or Rob. This kept her amused and ensured Bubby didn't totally win the day. As the new recruit to the gang it was interesting to observe the interactions between that pair and to spend time planning my future moves to ensure my elevation to top dog at a very young age. I had already worked out that speed would be my best asset and that, coupled with my high IQ level, would go somewhat to guaranteeing I could outmanoeuvre them both.

Stick throwing over and we were on the move again. We retraced our steps back along the Bay Road. Coco and Bubby remained off the lead and ran around in and out the reeds and jumped in the deep pools of water on the nature reserve which had been left by the retiring tide. It looked like lots of fun that I would soon get to join in with. I just had to win Amy and Rob over through 'behaving appropriately at all times and following all instructions to the letter' just like I would be expected to do if I were a pupil in Amy's class. However it was a known fact that a teacher's child was never as well behaved as expected and therefore why should I be an exception to that rule? We all knew that rules were meant to be broken otherwise they wouldn't have been invented. Now, I just had to persuade them that I was a fast learner of rules and get myself off this lead and running with the bad dogs, I mean big dogs.

As we approached the end of the Bay Road Coco and Bubby were hooked up to their leads in readiness for crossing the main coastal road. It was still a bright and sunny afternoon and there would be plenty opportunity for me to race round the garden on returning home - after I had had my tea of course! As I thought about what awaited me at home my saliva started to froth out the side of my floppies and I started to drool profusely; all this whilst still continuing to walk, proving I could multi-task. Rob noticed and made a passing comment about the excitement of my longer

a lab report

walk igniting my juices in preparation for my dinner. Amy laughed at his comment so I rubbed my face along the side of her trousers as pay back for mocking me again - now becoming a regular occurrence. What was wrong with preparing ahead of schedule when you appreciate your food?

We had crossed the road now and were on the home straight; as we headed down the brae I spotted a small bird fluttering around in one of the neighbour's bushes, so unannounced made a mad dash for it, wrapping the lead round Amy's legs and causing her to fall to the ground in one fell swoop. I stopped in my tracks, the decision was instantaneous; it was the bird or Amy. In my infinite wisdom I chose the bird. As I was now free of my lead having slipped my collar, I tore around the bush chasing the chaffinch from branch to branch, and jumping up trying to gnash it. Eventually, after taunting me, it flew off and simultaneously Amy flew at me, grabbing my scruff, sweeping me in to her arms, along with a 'BD' comment (I always abbreviate the 'Bad Dog' remark as it lessens its meaning for me when put in to just two meagre letters). I started licking Amy's face exuberantly as my way of sooking big time to lessen my chances of being given a mega telling off. I still got one though. I wondered if she would operate under the trial and retribution mode and give me a dinner that wouldn't even feed a sparrow? She need not bother as it was that silly lead's fault that had caused her to fall. It was just unfortunate that I happened to be attached to it at that particular moment in time.

j s carle

8

Getting Lost At Yellowcraigs

I was nearly sixteen weeks old and was about to be taken on my first ever walk outwith the surroundings of my own locality. We were all suitably kitted out in our collars, with name tags and mobile phone numbers - not my own personal mobile number as I didn't take it with me on walks in case I lost it in the long grasses or reeds or it got water logged when I swam in the sea - I also wouldn't want contacted on my walk to let me know Amy or Rob had gone missing and have to back-track to go and pick them up; that would ruin my adventures.

It was the beginning of July and the summer holidays had just started. Rob had taken two weeks of annual leave to

a lab report

be able to spend some time with us all so we could go out and about a bit more. This day Rob thought it would be good to go to a beautiful beach called Yellowcraigs down our way in East Lothian. Apparently it had a stunning lighthouse, picturesque views across to the Bass Rock, which was a beautiful white colour courtesy of the seagulls' poops. Why are mine brown and theirs white? An interesting phenomenon but I guess it must have been something to do with what they consume. What do gulls eat? Insects, fish, and...rubbish that they found in and on the ground. We have an uncanny similarity in our eating patterns then. I would have to refer to Wikipedia when I got home to research this as it is well known for its ability to answer obscure questions. A few quick searches on my front pad, I mean iPad, and I'd be the font of all knowledge.

We were now winging our way, or should I say, motoring our way along the coast road to Yellowcraigs. We passed through a small village called Gullane. I guessed this was where all the seagulls lived. How cool to have a place named after you I thought. I couldn't even claim that Labrador was named after me given that Coco arrived on this planet before me so it was obviously named after her.

As we reached the far end of this village the countryside opened up to rolling hills on the right, called the Lammermuirs, and on the left, I spotted a Kestrel sitting on a fence post at the side of one of the fields. I have eighty/eighty vision (humans have twenty/twenty and mine is a least four times as good), supersonic hearing, especially relative to the opening of fridge doors or crisp packets, and my ability to smell anything be it food, pheasant, bunny, bird, squirrel or food (just wanted to re-emphasise the food part again) is phenomenal at even a long range.

There was a ticking noise coming from the front of the car now and Rob took a sharp left down a very narrow tarmac road which led to a massive car park. He pulled in and parked up in the middle of a grassy area and away from any other form of civilisation. Bubby and Coco started bouncing around in the back excitedly and just about stomped on my head a few times. I squeezed myself over to the edge of the boot to avoid injury to my sylph-like body. They were making whining noises and I gathered from their enthusiasm that we were in for a treat.

Rob and Amy opened their car doors and strode around to the back of the car where Rob pressed the lever to open up the boot door, which sprang upwards immediately. Amy's hand was thrown forward inside to catch me before I had the slightest opportunity to bolt for the open space. My older, uglier sisters had already ejected themselves at this point, started chasing each other around on the grass and had then headed over to see some other dogs in the car park. Rob had pursued them, caught up with them, slipped on their leads and was hauling them back to the car to collect me. As the Queen would say, they were 'not amused'.

In the meantime Amy had attached my lead to my collar and had popped me on the ground in front of her feet as she closed up the car. As she did so she placed her foot through the handle of my lead, taking no chances of me escaping. Funny how she had so little faith in me; it was quite alarming really as I hadn't been too badly

a lab report

behaved on my lead and it had been two weeks since I had last pulled her over. She needed to learn to trust me to get the respect back. Surely a teacher should know the basic principles behind such practices. Never mind. Today I would forgive her as she had brought me somewhere new to play. However I am sure she would have thought twice about it if she had the slightest inkling relating to the drama which was about to unfold.

All together we crossed over the road which led from the car park to the woods. Once on the tree-lined path Coco and Bubby were released like greyhounds from their tracks and they sprinted deep in to Narnia. The track was still muddy from days of rain even though it was a warm, sunny summer's day today. Although I was still attached to my umbilical cord, I did my best to wade in to all the wettest, deepest, muddiest puddles I could as we proceeded along the path. Even though I came from the show dog line I tended to rebel against the need to remain clean and pristine at all times. Dogs are not supposed to be pampered pooches with hair ludicrously back combed to look like Coco the Clown at some performing circus or to have pompoms tied around their legs to stop them getting muddy. Dogs are supposed to be dogs and I just adored getting down with the dirt and interacting with the environment - unlike that wimpy dog Coco. I had to laugh on a few occasions, as I watched Coco further up the track, picking her way through the driest routes, ensuring her little paws didn't get dirty or wet. She called herself a gun dog. I could imagine Coco saying,

"I am sorry I can't fetch your pheasant for you as the ground is too muddy."

She would be laughed off the planet by the other gun dogs. I think we had obviously been born in to the wrong bodies. Slithering around in the mud and running through the puddles at pace so the dirt flicked up on my face and lined my whiskers was the best fun ever. I liked looking like some warrior who had gone to battle and won. I didn't worry that I looked like some dog that an owner would hate to have back in their car never mind their house. I did worry though that, alas, with the maquette brown all over my coat I could possibly be mistaken for a brown Labrador! Coco however looked untarnished and ready to strut her stuff on the catwalk, or should I say 'dog walk' alongside the real Coco Chanel; not that she was as pretty as me, as I've said before. I have it all. Looks, intelligence and the ability to have fun with a capital F.

At the end of the woods, we caught up with the big dogs and all five of us walked together towards the dunes. I could smell the sea air and was immensely excited with sheer anticipation as to what lay over the horizon and to get my first sighting of an expansive sandy beach. Bubby had veered off on an alternative route across a parallel dune and Coco was a few clean footsteps in front of us. We now had about five strides to go to reach the top of the dune and then I would be able to launch myself down the slope at the other side and race out to the sea which lay straight ahead. Knowing that Coco would show me the way, Amy turned to Rob and said,

"I am just going to take Rosie off her lead now. She should be fine just to follow Coco over the dune and down the other side. She's Coco's shadow and follows her everywhere. We couldn't have done this with any of our other dogs but she should be

a lab report

absolutely fine."

Rob agreed - so there I was, off trailing in Coco's wake as she powered across and down the other side of the dune. Amy and Rob reached the top of the dune and Coco appeared at their side.

"Where's Rosie?" Coco was asked.

No sign of me anywhere as I had my own agenda after being on the lead for the last twenty minutes.

Now the rest is all news to me but I will tell you the story as it unfolded and has been re-told to others since this day. What I would like to say is that the moral of this story is not about 'how not to trust your puppy off the lead at an early age' but, is instead, to show what amazing homing techniques us Labradors have and how our finely-honed sense of smell and inbuilt tracking device, can get us safely back to base.

Here is what happened in my absence:

"Rosie, Rosie."

Amy and Rob were screeching at the top of their voices. They were asking Coco and Bubby where I was. I am sure Coco knew where I was, or should I say, she did know as she saw me head off in the wrong direction but did nothing to right me. She obviously thought desperate times require desperate measures and losing me would help her ploy to return to the top dog position. Nasty trick to play, Coco Loco.

"Rosie, Rosie," shouted Amy, but to no avail.

"She could be anywhere. I think we should split up as we will have more chance of finding her. Keep your mobile phone on and if you find her let me know ASAP. I'll go this way," Rob pointed along the east end of the beach towards North Berwick.

"I'll go this way," Amy said pointing across the dunes and along the west way of the beach.

Coco and Bubby accompanied Amy and Rob went off on his own. Amy ran around frantically, asking everyone she came across the same question,

"Have you seen a black Labrador puppy? She's only fourteen weeks old and she's gone missing near here." She got the same answer every time, which was a 'No'.

Rob was getting nowhere fast either and twenty minutes later I still hadn't been found. Worse still, in their haste to find me, half-deaf Bubby had also gone astray.

Meeting back together at the spot they had last seen me it was time to put Plan B in to action. Rob decided it might be sensible to retrace his way back to the car, in the hope, for some mad reason, that I had done the same. He was doubtful but thought it was worth a try anyway. Amy was now tearful, alluding to the possibility that in this hinterland it was unlikely they would ever find me again and she couldn't bear going home without me. She said she would search until sun down and thereafter in the dark if that's what it took to locate me (how heroic - but I am absolutely worth it).

Amy stayed put to look for Bubby and Rob took Coco with him for fear of her running off somewhere too - the last thing they needed to happen right at this moment in time to add to their already heightened stress.

"Bubby, Bubby," Amy cried out, in an ever-increasing

a lab report

panicked voice.

The beach walkers must have thought she had totally lost the plot. She had now even changed the name she was calling. Losing one dog was incompetent, mislaying two was a case of gross negligence if I do say so myself. What sort of a family had I been adopted in to?

Just at that point Bubby peered her head round one of the grassy bushes, looking totally unperturbed by the happenings and the distress both she and me were causing. Flinging her arms around her, Amy squeezed her tightly and gave her a big kiss on the forehead in sheer relief,

"One down, one to go," muttered Amy. "Did you see Rosie on your travels Bubs? We need to keep hunting for her. Let's see if we can find her together. Do you want to try barking to see if she recognises your call?"

She flicked a rope lead over Bubby's neck and they started their search, again, of the dunes, calling out my name every step of the way. They switched between running, walking and jogging and even though they were tiring, neither gave up their quest to find me. Sweat cascaded like a waterfall down the inside of Amy's trouser legs and top and she wiped her brow regularly to stop it running in to her eyes. With the excessive perspiration and all the exercise she now resembled a Belisha Beacon. A great asset if I had been looking to find her in the dark! Bubby was doing her impression of the black 'panter' getting a bit hot under the collar trying to keep up with Amy, as at thirteen years old, she was not as sprightly as she used to be and being the lady she was, endurance running was never her thing. Come to think of it, neither was exercise in a big way!

Amy's phone started to ring. She stopped immediately and hunted in her trouser pockets, pulling her phone out, her hands shaking as she did so. She fumbled for the button to answer it. She appeared apprehensive about doing so as she knew the call would bring either good or unwanted news.

"Hello, Rob?" Amy's voice was full of trepidation.

"I've found her."

"Where?" she asked inquisitively, at the same time as dropping to her knees on the sand beneath her. She was physically exhausted and emotionally drained.

"When I arrived at the car I saw these four small paws underneath it and there she was."

Amy laughed out loud with over-whelming disbelief, "How could she have navigated her way back that distance? That's amazing! I am on my way back now. You'll be pleased to know I found Brambles too. See you in ten minutes or so."

That was their version of events of how I was found. For me it had been a little less dramatic but nonetheless an interesting adventure.

After accidentally on purpose ditching Coco Channel, I mean Chanel, I had headed back to the woods to play in the puddles and make more of a splash. Being on a lead was restricting and it had been so much more fun running and jumping in them with no one there to get on my case about getting overly dirty. I would line myself up with the puddles and run full pelt at them, and on take-

a lab report

off I could be heard shouting 'Geronimo' as I landed smack in the middle of the deepest section. The wetter and dirtier I got the more hyper I became, until eventually I looked like I had visited the local spa resort for a full body mud bath. The plus point was I would have a beautiful soft, silky coat when it eventually washed off.

After about ten minutes of self-play and suitably grubby, and in disguise with the local environment in my brown tan, I headed back to the car park where I found a half full bag of crisps (notice I am ever the optimist or I would have phrased this as half empty) and gobbled them up along with their foil wrapper. The gammon flavour kept making me burp for a few minutes afterwards but my tummy soon settled. I would need to write to the crisp manufacturers as I had enjoyed the crisps but felt the wrapper lacked a bit in flavour and the texture was quite rough on the roof of my mouth. (Giving birth to it the next day also proved quite onerous. I had tried to free myself of it by pulling my bottom along on the grass hoping it would come out itself. No such joy! Rob eventually had to help me by getting a tissue to pluck the rest from my raw bottom as I had started to take a crazy turn in the garden as I became demented with it.)

I then wandered down the car park to the ice cream van; it didn't seem to be serving anyone one or anything without money, but the remnants of a dropped cone between the van and the visitor toilets seemed to suffice to let me have my first experience of a Mister Whippy ice cream. Now my belly was sufficiently full I decided to head back to the car. I had been amazed that nobody had taken any time to speak to me en route through the woods or in the car park -this seemingly homeless, lonesome, adorable little puppy. Normally I was swamped with attention being the stunningly pretty pup that I am. As I had predicted earlier this must have been because they thought I was a brown Lab.

As I awaited the return of my new family from their walk, it had never occurred to me that there was anything untoward going on or that they would have been overly concerned about my disappearance. It wasn't until Rob arrived at the car, with Coco in tow, and saw me leaning nonchalantly against one of our car tyres, that his elated and yet exasperated voice was the first hint of anything having been up. He picked me and squeezed me tightly, kissing my head.

"Rosie. Am I glad to find you! We thought we'd lost you forever." I glanced down at Coco and gave her that 'unlucky pal' look at the same time as smiling as broadly as I could, with bits of cone filling the gaps between my puppy teeth.

A phone call to Amy and within ten minutes we were all reunited, with everyone happy as can be that I was found safe and well. I pretended to look a little stressed and forlorn from the day's events in the hope that they would know that stress burns calories and that I would require a bigger tea that evening to replace what I had metabolised. Rob and Amy needed to understand how the far-reaching trauma of being abandoned had affected me and how it might continue to do so for the foreseeable future. I was sure I could milk this event for some time to come. Take a bow. A second Oscar Award nominee performance. I was getting so good. Disney would be scouring the papers for me as I spoke. I could see my

a lab report

name in lights at the Cannes Film Festival. Best actress: Rosie Posie. I would stroll down the red carpet, 'posing' for photographs and stamping autographs. That would be the life...

All the way back in the car they reiterated the story of searching for me and how bereft they would have been had they not found me. They discussed the contingency plan they were going to put in to place next had I still been missing after an hour. Apparently I had managed to find my way back over a mile and a half to the car park which for a pup my age was phenomenal. Well tell me something I didn't know! What a stir I had caused. What excitement I had brought to their life and day. What a talking point!

Unfortunately for me the upshot of it all was a cold hosing on return to the house to fire off the mud on my body. Brrr........it was icy cold! I had to shake myself from nose to tail to expel the water from my coat to help me dry off and let my coat shine black again. The one positive from my mammoth escapade was I did get a rather large bowl of food. Yum. Just as well for me they didn't know what I had eaten until the passing of my crisp wrapper the following day!

j s carle

9

The Golf Course

This became my staple walk for the next few months following my vanishing act at Yellowcraigs; now you see me, now you don't. Abracadabra, alacazam, am... a m a z i n g! I felt I was being unfairly punished for the perilous danger my owners had placed me in by slipping my lead off to run across the dunes with that poor guide of a dog they called Coco. It should be her getting Community Service for pulling such a stunt which could have resulted in me going missing infinitum. According to all the dog training books I have read it is always the owners' fault and never the dog's; although I would debate that on this occasion as I would say cuckoo Coco was as equally to blame as Rob and

a lab report

Amy. Notwithstanding this issue, I liked these books as they spoke with accuracy and conviction and unwittingly always took the side of us dogs who were forced to carry out such heinous crimes as stealing objects, eating rubbish and pooing right in front of people enjoying their picnics, encouraging them to ditch their half-eaten sandwiches in disgust, only for us to hoover them up to ensure the maintenance of the environment. Timing was everything and paramount to the crime and the best of us knew exactly how to play our cards right to maximise our rewards.

Given owners are responsible for our behaviour this gave me a free licence to do absolutely anything, within reason, and for Amy or Rob to cop the blame. Superboss. This being the case I would make sure I used my get out of jail card for worthwhile crimes and then sit back and enjoy the ensuing entertainment. The golf course therefore provided an ample opportunity to put these concepts to the test and see how golfers would react to my aiding their play - in all of its manifestations!

As Amy and Rob walked the golf course most days they were well known by the green keepers and most of the regular golfers. Many remarked on how well behaved Coco and Brambles were; standing watching the golfers as they would tee off and sitting patiently as they putted out. Model pupils.

Then I arrived to rock the boat!

Initially I was kept on the lead for the majority of the walk, only getting off as we neared the beach at the far end. As my recall improved with the use of treats, I was afforded more and more time off the lead as my natural homing device was inextricably linked to food. I was taught to stand to attention and salute golfers as they tee-d off and to sit and wait as golfers putted out. More treats. I observed Coco at work as she sniffed in the rough to find balls and each time she returned one to Rob or Amy, she would be rewarded with a treat. I was smart enough to do that too so joined in her excavations and if I failed to come up with a find myself and she did, I would pinch hers and pop it in my mouth then race back to Amy and Rob, dropping it in front of them to proclaim how clever I was. I would then be rewarded for my industrious efforts. That notion again: Coco was my barking dog and worked hard for little return. On a good day me and Coco could find about eight balls in the rough and, being the generous people they were, Amy and Rob would pass on these balls to golfers playing along the course; all part of the peace making process and keeping the golfers on side for any menacing stunts I would pull in the future –of which there would be many!

Me and Coco were relatively popular with golfers who would call on our finely honed skills to assist in searching for a lost ball in the rough. Amy and Rob tried to show off when they commanded us to 'go seek'. More often than not one of us would come up trumps and we'd both get a treat for looking even if the other had found the ball; so I never tried too hard knowing what the outcome was: it was a win/win situation. Our search and rescue skills were even more useful when a ball had landed down on the coastal rocks and we were sent to fetch it and carry it back over the rough terrain. I manoeuvred so gracefully I was poetry in motion and golfers were astonished at my skill when they watched me in

a lab report

action. They were always extremely grateful to us for the return of their expensive balls (I was very selective in my retrievals and never picked up the cheaper makes if I did find them as I firmly believed they were what had caused the poor play in the first instance). Coco and I had developed celebrity status and golfers often asked after us if they met Rob and Amy out walking without us when they were doing their wildlife photography. Why they didn't take me with them on this outing I don't know as I had a great appreciation of nature too.

Nobody taught me much about what happened in between a tee-off and putting-out and that was probably the first time I was to get Amy in to trouble when she was on the receiving end of a woman whose feathers had been a bit ruffled when I had run after her ball and half inched it as it rolled down the fairway after she had just driven off. Picking up a ball in play was allegedly very different from retrieving a lost one from the rough. How did one differentiate? That was 'ruff'. A ball was a ball after all wasn't it?

Amy had done her utmost to put things right, when I had eventually given my grand theft ball up, by surreptitiously replacing it back at approximately the same spot it had landed at. However the 'eagle' eyed woman had noticed this endeavour and had marched at a frighteningly fast pace towards her, where she had given her an earful about my lack of training and the fact that I was off my lead. No amount of explaining I was a puppy in training made any headway towards making things more palatable for the women. Amy continued to apologise profusely and the woman eventually backed down a little saying it was 'okay on this occasion' but if it had been 'a medal' it would have annulled her game. I nearly laughed out my hairy little coat. With the distance she was hitting there was no way she was going to get any medal, and certainly not a gold one. With the extra metres I had added to her ball's flight path she should have bitten my paws off in gratefulness as I may have assisted eagle eyes in achieving a birdie! Tweet, tweet.

On this occasion my get-out-of jail card had stayed firmly in my coat pocket as I didn't think this incident merited the use of it; it was more like a chance card as I had certainly monopolised the situation.

I did choose to use my card at a later stage; as a stay-in-jail card as I reckoned that I was safer behind bars after what I had done. It was a dreich day and there had not been many players on the course so I had been allowed to walk off my lead most of the way round the walk. It wasn't until the final green, before we descended to the beach, that we came across three Irishmen about to putt out. I knew they were Irish as I had heard that lovely Irish lilt as they spoke to each other, and I had fallen head over heels in love with their accents and, unfortunately for one of them, with his furry club-head cover that he had just laid down seconds earlier at the side of the green. It was a bright green frog with big eyes and a red tongue hanging out. I was quick off the mark, followed by a screech from Amy to the said gentleman,

"Excuse me; watch your club head cover!"

The request came all too late and I had skidded in and swept it up in my soft, slaver clad mouth and was now taunting everyone

a lab report

by running back and fore across the green clicking past the other balls as I went. One of the men joined in my game by trying to chase after me and grab it out my mouth. "Far too slow mister snail," I sang out through the small gaps at the side of my mouth as I sped off past him ready to take on my next opponent. Amy was now on her knees at the side of the green, perhaps praying, who knows? She was calling out to me to come, to return to her - trying to entice me with loads of treats which filled her cupped hands - but I had something far more valuable at this moment in time and no-way-hosey was I going to pass this up that easily for some measly treats. I stopped at the far side of the green, popped Mr Ribbit down long enough to give them false hope indeed that the game was now over. A moment hung in time and I stared from face to face. I smiled wryly.

"Good girl Rosie," summoned Amy.

Pouncing on Kermit and flicking him upwards, I scrunched him in to my cavern and then, feeling like I had a frog in my throat, which I did, spat him out high in to the sky. As he fell to earth, or grass, I trapped him with my paws and like a mad dog, which I was, started to rip him open like some Christmas parcel. Amy was now starting to sound desperate and was literally crawling across the green commando style trying to reach me un-noticed. I shook froggy around a bit more and as it had now played dead, was sufficiently covered in slavers (so much so that I was beginning to have trouble gripping it properly myself), I ditched him and decided to return to Amy to take her up on her earlier offer of the treats. As if coordinated with my actions, Amy flew past me to rescue the remnants of Monsieur Frog. Picking him up and wiping him vigorously on her trousers and fleece, and ignoring the torn section, she cleaned it up as best as possible and handed it back to Murphy. I guess that was his name as I knew all Scots, except for Rob, were called Jock, weren't they? So I had deduced all Irish men had to be called Murphy. I knew a dog called Murphy who had Irish owners so my thought processing did make sense!

Anyway, Murphy thanked Amy for returning his mottled club cover and stuck it back on to his caddy without examining it in too great a detail. At least by the time he did, I would be long gone. He would reflect on this as being one of his most memorable events whilst on his trip to Scotland and I knew my exploits would be recounted to many a friend and provide a source of great amusement to others on his return to Ireland. Or did he live in Scotland? If he were to return to play my local golf course again (I do hope I hadn't put him off) I would suggest he gets neoprene covers for his clubs as they did not absorb slavers as much and I don't like the texture in my mouth so he would have got it back a lot sooner.

When Amy returned to me I was sitting pretty at the side of the green alongside Bubby and Coco, who had taken no part in my game. She removed my lead from over her shoulder and looped it around my neck, pulling it tightly; an attempt to choke me I think. I coughed and spluttered but received no sympathy from her and even the golfers pretended not to hear me as they finished putting out. In my defence, if people are going to bring furry toys to the golf course and then lay them out on the grass, how can a pup be expected to walk on by without saying hello?

a lab report

Although Amy had been mortified by my behaviour, and if the ground could have swallowed her up I am sure she would have thanked it for doing so, she did find some humour in the story when she retold it to Rob on his return from work. He said that I wouldn't have done that if he had been there; really I thought? Was that an invitation? I decided to see what I could do to have a little fun at his expense so as we headed out our next walk I grabbed George the monkey and took him with me as my companion. Eventually I got fed up carrying him and dropped him about ten minutes in to our hour long walk. This left Rob carrying George for the remainder of the walk, making him look like some deranged teenager in the eyes of bewildered adults we passed en route. One up!!

j s carle

10

Getting Dressed

My worst nightmare was about to be realised and come to fruition. It was now September and I was six months old and at the vets to be 'dressed'. I had managed to resist the need to wear clothes and bling; I liked the 'au natural' look as I had no need to cover myself up with tango tans or dye my hair blonde to look like one of these golden Labradors. I wondered therefore what 'getting dressed' actually meant.

I believe that this colloquial phrase was used instead of the medical term 'spayed', which means the equivalent of a hysterical, or something like that, which in turn means removing my ovaries so I could not have a litter. Amy had told me that the vet would make

a lab report

a small incision in my belly, remove my bits, and then stick me back together with surgical glue or sew me up. This would be a fairly similar procedure to the one I saw Amy perform on some of my toys when the stuffing had fallen out through a tear in their skin or coat, and she removed the bits hanging out, then sewed it back together to look as good as new. They seemed neither up nor down from the procedure, so I guessed it would be the same for me.

My owners had been advised that they could not pup me anyway as I was not breed standard with my two missing teeth. Even though I would not be producing puppies, which would give me a saggy belly anyway so I was not overly perturbed by missing out on that, it was appropriate to take precautions and have me dressed just in case some handsome sire decided to try and have his wicked way with me. Which was highly probable given how devastatingly attractive I am.

Checked in, I was kissed goodbye on the forehead and hugged tightly by Amy before being led through, by Rosie, my favourite vet nurse, to the back of the surgery to the preparation and recovery suite. It was daunting as I had never been parted from my family before and was unsure what lay ahead. I was unimpressed by being coerced, by my namesake, in to what they termed a 'kennel' yet I would have referred to as a cage. No five star luxury in this joint. It was only made a little more bearable, because I was young, I had been allowed to take a toy in with me as a comforter, so I had taken Coco's monkey George.

This would mean that she would miss both me and him. Ha, ha! As George was much bigger than me, he took up most of the space in my cage, and I had to clamber on top of him to flatten him to make sufficient space for me. On hindsight I should have brought Vinny van Patch instead, who was significantly smaller, but I needed him to stay at home and spy on the on-goings there, which he would report back to me about on my safe return that evening. Having George alongside me as my bouncer, with all these strange dogs and cats peering at me in my cage seemed a good idea. Vinny wouldn't have had the same presence as George, not that either of them looked particularly fierce. However his chewed up ear could have given off the impression that he was a bit of a fighter and not one to be crossed.

As I waited for my fate I stared from cage to cage. I could eyeball any of the animals as there was a level of safety behind them there bars! One dog looked pretty gruff and had a metal spiky studded collar on. I think he was a Chihuahua. Not to be messed with was the message intended but his sheer size made that message a very mixed one. I wondered what my chewed up collar adoring my neck said about me? Pity probably!

I continued with my cage review. They were all filled today and had either dogs, cats or some nondescript, weird-looking animals in them that I didn't know the names of - probably another breed of cat. Some of the dogs burled round and round in their cages and barked. Others were sleeping soundly. Others were joining in a dawn chorus, which sounded like a pack of howling wolves. I tried to join in but couldn't match their pitch. As I saw Rosie pass my cage I let out a sharp bark and wagged my tail, begging her to come and speak to me or let me out - or both.

a lab report

In what seemed like a lifetime later, Rosie came and plucked me out my cage, attached my lead to my collar and took me out to a small section of grass at the back of the surgery. She encouraged me to go pee and poo. This was standard procedure before any surgery to try and get one to empty one's bowels so one did not do so on the operating table half way through surgery. Perish the thought! Anyway, I did this quite easily as I was nervous and things tended to flow quite openly when I was in this mode. Once finished, I was led back in to one of the consulting rooms and Lucy, my vet, lifted me up on to the table. Whilst Rosie cuddled me Lucy stabbed a massive jag in to my bahookie. I flinched a little as she did so even though it felt very similar to some of the nips Coco gave me when we played. This was called my 'pre-med' and was intended to calm me down and take the edge off my nervous energy prior to my operation.

I was then taken back to my cage to allow the drug time to take effect and after a very short time I felt 'totally chilled out man'. It must have been about an hour later when Rosie returned to collect me and take me through to the surgical room. Pooped up, oops, popped up on the table, Rosie cuddled me again. For some reason, I knew what was coming. Oh no, it was an electric razor like the one I saw Rob use in the mornings on his face. I squirmed to try and free myself. No way was Lucy shaving my facial hair so I looked like some weirdo dog; on second thoughts, with a shaved face, who would know I was even a dog? Rosie held me tighter and the razor came ever closer. Lucy was now shaving a strip of hair off my lower right leg and as soon as she had finished, she ditched the razor, and without a moment to lose, picked up a jag and inserted the needle in to my bald patch and pumped some fluid in to me. The rest was all a blur on the landscape and I have no recollection of what happened, except enjoying running through the fields chasing Coco and Bubby.

The next thing I remember was a face peering in my cage, repeatedly calling my name.

"Rosie... Rosie... Can you hear me...? Rosie..."

I half opened my eyes to see two Rosies staring in at me - had she duplicated in my absence? Hands were now reaching in to my cage and stroking my coat gently. Was this what a hangover felt like? If so, I never wanted to become a dogaholic.

Why was Rosie calling my name? Why was my belly rumbling? What had happened to me? Oh yes, I remembered. I had my stuffing ripped out and I had been sewn back together again.

I dozed off to sleep again and must have slept for a good few hours before Rob came to pick me up just after six pm. He was taken in to the consulting room then I was brought through to meet him on my lead. Although I was over the moon to see him I was still a little drowsy so after wagging my tail a bit and having an accidental leak on the floor, I lay down gingerly beside his feet and shut my eyes as Lucy went over the post-operative instructions. He was advised on my eating, walks - which were to be lead only until my stitches had dissolved - my antibiotics, painkillers and generally looking after my wound and ensuring it was kept clean. No licking. I loved licking. How else would I keep clean? I couldn't imagine Coco or Brambles doing that job for me and having my

a lab report

coat smell of their halitosis breaths.

Lucy held up 'An Elizabethan Collar', which she explained would stop me licking my wound and opening it up or infecting it. Quelle horreur! It would look like a traffic cone had been stuck on my head (I had seen drunk people wear them on their heads in films) and I knew that my motor skills were not yet finely tuned enough to ensure that I would not take everyone and sundry with me as I went, if I was forced to wear one. They were also not the easiest things to eat with, although acted as a good bib if you dropped anything; it made it hard to get your mouth down to your bowl to get stuck in to your nosh. To all intents and purposes it was the equivalent of a gastric band and could be a cheap alternative to surgery for all these overweight dogs - another pioneering suggestion of mine. Luckily for me, Rob said Amy would be keeping an eye on me night and day so I wouldn't need one and if he did, he could always nip back for one. Whew - A lucky escape!

Before any more obscene suggestions were given, I clambered to my feet and made ready to go. Lucy asked to see me back in a week's time to check my progress but if there were any concerns at all, just to bring me straight back up. After folding up the instruction leaflet and shoving it in his trouser pocket, Rob picked up my lead, thanked Lucy, who had butchered me, and we exited the consulting room and headed straight out the surgery to the car. Apparently Rob had paid my fees on the way in to save me hanging around in my tender state. Imagine having to pay for being mutilated.

I was encouraged by Rob to walk to the car. I still felt drunk and a bit shaky on my feet, and the world seemed to spin around about me. My pace was in keeping with a tortoise, which I think I had seen in one of the cages along from me. Why would anyone want one of them as a pet? I would be shell shocked if I was given one! I'd rather have the hare as at least we could play chasey.

When we got to the car, Rob lifted me in to my bed in the boot and tucked me up in a cosy blanket. Cosie, Rosie, Posie. Just as we were reversing out the space there was a knock at Rob's window. It was Rosie. What did she want?

"I am really sorry but we forgot to give you Rosie's monkey before you left," she said, brandishing George. "We just totally forgot to take him out her kennel when we were bringing her back through to you."

'Rosie's monkey'. Even though I was exhausted I clocked the part 'Rosie's monkey'. He was now mine because Rosie said so. Coco would not be pleased.

When we arrived back home, Rob carried me inside, still in my bed, to save me having to crawl out and walk again. I could get quite used to being catered for. This was the height of indulgence. He placed my bed down in the hallway and my sisters were allowed to greet me ever so gently. I remained in my bed, which Amy then carried through to the living room and placed in front of the fire. Rob pulled my post-operative instructions out of his pocket and passed these over to Amy so she could digest these.

"She's to be kept warm and quiet tonight. She can have a light tea in a few hours, if she wants to eat, and when she goes out to the garden, she needs to be on her lead," he recounted.

a lab report

Curled up and toastie in my bed at the fireside, I fell off to sleep, whining and howling intermittently as my anaesthetic continued to wear off. I actually slept so soundly that I skipped my dinner and was only woken up to be lifted out to the garden for a quick liquid stop and then returned to my bed to zzzzzzzzzz... All night through.

Feeling much better the next morning, I had a delicious, gourmet-breakfast of fish and rice, that was really quite nice and certainly filled a hole in my very rumbly tummy, which was almost concave as I hadn't eaten for so long. I would certainly need to make up for lost food over the coming days but not so much as to swell my belly and cause my stitches to pop open like one of my stuffed toys. Not that it was a major concern given I had my own seamstress on site.

11

Obedience Training

So there I was, seven months old and walking up the road to my first obedience class with Rob. I had been enrolled on the six week Kennel Club's Bronze course being held at the local church hall on Tuesday evenings. Sacre bleu - why the Kirk offered to host training for skittery, incontinent puppies (not me as I was now well beyond that stage) in such a place I would never know.

Allegedly if I did well on this course I would be able to progress to the next level of silver! I would need to see what I could do to sabotage this as there was no way I was going to some musty old hall, to walk round and round on my lead as we all eye-balled each other (owners included) to ascertain who was king

a lab report

pin. I had better things to do of an evening than partake in such trivia. I mean. . . what dog in the world likes obedience? It's the equivalent of being sent to a canine reform school for trainers to impose a set of learned behaviours on impressionable puppies. Pity that wasn't me! I knew everything there was to know without attending; walking my walk wasn't necessarily the same as talking the talk, if they were to reference Rob or Amy. Nobody needed to show me how to eat, sit, lie down, walk to heel (did biting the foot at the same time count as heel walking), stay, go pee or poo. I fully comprehended 'leave' but just chose not to obey such commands. I understood 'good dog' and paid no heed to 'bad dog' as negative reinforcement of bad behaviour was not deemed appropriate. I had read that in one of my canine books about training the human.

Tonight I had my plush bone collar on. Attached to this was a short, nylon type lead, which was not nearly as nice as my soft, pliable, fleecy one that gave when I pulled. Much less manoeuvrability on this lead for nonsense - more's the pity.

After paying our six weeks' training fees to the lady sitting at the table at the entrance door, who also gave me a telling off for putting my front paws up on her table to say hello, and a further reprimand to Rob for failing to have me sufficiently under control, we proceeded to the main hall where we were requested to stand in a space, away from other dogs. Bored, and on the understanding that these classes were about socialisation, I pulled sternly on my lead and dragged Rob over so I could go and speak to Leila, who was a trainee guide dog puppy. She smiled at me like my sisters used to do. She then snapped her jaws open and closed like some giant crane and I thought she was going to eat me up. Either she hadn't been fed before she came or I looked good enough to eat. I decided not to put it to the acid test. Her owner gave her a row for being horrid to me; just as well as guide dogs are supposed to be placid at all times or she would risk not graduating as one.

I had encountered a number of guide-dogs when I had graced them with my presence at a charity fund raising event back in the summer, when I was only four and three quarter months old. There had been a variety of fun, and more serious competitions you could enter which were judged by the Kennel Club. Coco signed up for waggiest tail and Best of Breed. Embarrassingly she never got a place in either. She did get a third place in the obedience trials, which had no bearing on looks and required little intelligence to complete the mundane tasks of 'sit, down, fetch and a basic recall'. If she couldn't do that with her eyes shut by the age of five she wasn't worth hanging out with. Hanging out with her anyway was debatable given her failing reputation after today. Brambles didn't come with us as she protested she was too old for entry to such humiliating events and having to wait around and watch us make fools of ourselves for little or no return. She was wrong on that account regarding me!

Now, as you know, I am never one to blow my own trumpet, but I secured second place in Best Puppy; not sure why I was not first but perhaps the judge had spotted (or not) my two missing teeth when she pulled up my jowls to look at my white gnashers. Being second in this competition allowed me to advance immediately to strut my stuff round the ring, with Rob, in Best-in-Show, where I

a lab report

was awarded third place - not bad for a first outing. It just all came so naturally to me coming from my long line of show champions and my ability to shine like a diamond amongst the lesser gems.

Glaringly jealous, Coco tried to denounce my rosettes on the way home by stressing that it was only a small, fun event and not to get ideas above my station. At least all her agility trophies had been won fair and square against all the tops dogs in Scotland. I puckered out my chest, stuck my nose in the air and treated her with the contempt she deserved. The green-eyed monster was a terrible thing, even though I knew she had brown eyes.

Back to training. As tonight was our first encounter with 'real' training our coach instructed our owners on grooming us (that sounds terrible nowadays doesn't it - so let's refer to it as brushing my coat and checking my ears and teeth), feeding us and the types of collars and leads to use. He stressed that choke-chain leads should never be used as they could hurt our necks. I didn't like the look of them anyway and associated them more with 'hard core' dogs like the one Bill Sykes owned in Oliver Twist. Wasn't he called Bullseye? Maybe he'd been hit by a dart at some point that he'd got a butch, tough name like that?

Once he'd gone thought the drivel we got on to the action. Well, when I say action, I mean walking round and round the hall one way, then when given a 'back', or 'left' command, our owners would turn us by their left shoulder, and continue to walk monotonously round and round the other way like I was some brain dead, robotic pooch. We were then taught 'sit', which I had been doing for months. Teach me something new I wanted to bawl. Amy would have cringed, as a teacher, about the lack of differentiation for the more able, like myself, in the class. No wonder we pups misbehaved, just like kids, when the tasks offered were well below our ability. This was torturous. Another five weeks looming of this mundaneness. Untenable.

An hour had passed and that was sufficient learning for us all for session one according to our trainer. Not that I had learnt anything except how to be borederer than bored, if that's a word? Tuesdays had now officially become the most dreaded day of my week. It was etched on my brain like some recurring nightmare, which it would become. I would chalk off each of my sessions on my chocolate calendar as humans do when they want to count down to exciting events like Christmas. This would be me counting down to its finish, which would be my own time for celebration.

Leila's mum was all for chatting to Rob but I was keen to escape this prison ASAP so sat down on the floor, lifted my back paws off the floor and performed a skid pull. You know the ones I mean that dogs do when we have an itch. Humans always become mortified when we do this and this was my best attempt to speed up our departure. It worked as Rob looked down at me and then stuck his boot, inadvertently where the sun don't shine, to lift up my bahookie and move me forwards in the direction of the door, saying politely to Leila's mum that we really needed to go. Freedom! I am going home.

When Rob was telling Amy about Leila after we got home from our session, she told him a story about one of her pupils at school who now owned a failed guide dog. Rob enquired how

a lab report

it had come to fail. Allegedly, the dog was on one of its final assessments to ascertain its suitability as a Guide Dog. It had been tasked with leading a blind folded tester through a well-known retail store, negotiating all the people, obstacles and coping with any distractions successfully or without reacting to them. It had been managing really well when tragedy struck. On passing a manikin, which adorned a fur coat, the dog started to bark, and then proceeded to jump on the dummy and rip off the faux fur coat, pulling it to shreds. For some unknown reason, it was thought the dog had perceived the manikin to be an intruder. That is, as her pupil had told her, was how he had come to own his lovely two year old Labrador, which had been their loss but his gain. Rob laughed loudly and then quirkily commented,

"And the moral of the story is... Don't wear fur coats."

Even I thought that was semi funny until I thought about what I wear every day. In retrospect, not so funny!

The next four weeks of training (week six was the test) was very repetitive, so we could 'groove in learning' the moves we needed to perform to a high level to pass. Getting me to the venue itself proved more and more challenging to Rob as well in advance of my time for departure for my class, I would hide out in different places around the house, or in my kennel in the garden, to avoid having to go. I did not win out. On the way up the road, I would try to jump the walls of local gardens in a desperate attempt to escape. I knew Rob was savvy enough to know I didn't want to go, but he kept telling me that I needed to attend; that it was good for me (?) as well as it being a pre-requisite for being allowed to attend agility training. So as I am altruistic, I continued to attend and give of my best. What else would I be doing on a Tuesday evening anyway? Possibly watching Wallace and Gromit. The only bonus of going to the obedience training was that I had made a few new friends, who were as equally turned off as I was. They were a collie called Murphy, who was very handsome with his tri-colour coat and also another Labrador called Mickey, as in mouse, who was black like me, and liked to have a good old carry on. He never failed to amuse me with his antics and was known in the local village for barking at strategic points when watching bowling matches - usually at the wrong times and for the benefit of the opposing teams. I had to remind myself that not all my breed were as gifted and intelligent as myself and I would keep coming back to Coco as proof of that claim.

The Test Night

Groomed, hosed after my walk, as I had rolled on a dead fish washed up at the beach, and raring to go, okay, slight exaggeration, I headed off to my test. How did I know it was my test? My calendar told me so. Week six! I had been warned by Rob to be on my best behaviour and to follow all of his instructions to the 'letter'. I'll have a P then please. Joking! I wouldn't let him down but wouldn't let him think I wouldn't or couldn't make decisions for myself.

The test started by the examiner coming round and speaking to us all individually. He stroked my coat, checked my eyes, looked in my ears, which smelt nicely of fresh, yellow wax, and

a lab report

then peered at my teeth. He had big hands and his breath stunk of garlic. Maybe he was a vampire? Or he had a cross to bear?

"Aren't you a bonnie lass?" he remarked.

Don't need to state the obvious I wanted to say. Everyone in the hall knew this. He then walked off to check out another comatose pooch.

Minutes later, our owners were asked to get their combs or brushes out and show him them grooming us. I did my usual of trying to bite the brush but Rob held me firmly, dragging the implement through my black, lush hair. It always tickled me and that's why I squirmed.

Next task, which was a group one, was to plod round the hall, walking your dog, on a relaxed lead, on your left and when he said swap, to change direction, quickly and efficiently whilst keeping us to heel. This was a skoosh, although I would have rather demonstrated this off the lead as I was even better at it this way. Perhaps show-offs were not allowed tonight.

One by one we were called forward by the tester to perform a sit, stay, on the lead and then off. This was then followed up by a down stay, on or off the lead - the owner could choose. The test culminated with a basic recall, off the lead.

Apart from a little excitement watching Murphy and Mickey perform their tasks, as Mickey ran straight to me on the recall, I was about falling asleep when I heard my name being called.

"Rosie Maxwell."

I had never heard my full name before and wasn't sure that I liked it. I was so used to thinking it was Rosie Posie, which was much more user friendly. Rob Posie. Perhaps he should change his name to suit mine as it sounded equally ludicrous.

I stepped forward like some criminal in an identity parade and walked up the middle of the hall towards the examiner, preparing my brain to do my tricks. Sit, stay and down were not a problem. Inherently I could be a bit of a lazy dog when given the opportunity and there had been little of interest to waken up my mind and challenge me so far this evening. I felt my lead being unhooked and the command 'stay' issued to me as Rob proceeded to walk down to the opposite end of the hall. It's time for the recall, which I had performed to an extremely high level on all previous occasions therefore Rob had no need to think it would be any different tonight. Why would it? There was no room for complacency though and what he had failed to realise was, as he headed down to the opposite end from me, I was trailing in his shadow and only a mere step behind him. When he reached the bottom and turned round, there I was. Surprise! Unimpressed, and without saying a word to me, he hooked me back up to my lead and marched me back to the top of the hall at pace, to start the task all over again. Mission accomplished, me at the top and him at the bottom, we were ready to perform our team recall.

"Rosie, come... Rosie... come," Rob encouraged from down the hall.

I sat staring at him, rooted to the spot. I was pooped. That meant for those of you who don't understand my phraseology, I was spent, out of energy, creamed, knackered and above all, bored.

"Rosie... come!" He was now bellowing the command and a

a lab report

little frustration was kicking in to his tone too.

Chill! I am on my way Master. Moving no faster than a dog on their way to obedience training, I made my way down towards him. A slow-motion button would have even speeded me up. I was however, totally under control. I saw Mickey out the corner of my eye, grinning from ear to ear and giving me a paws-up for my performance. I was so laid back I would soon be horizontal. That sounded good if it had been in front of the fire at home. When I finally reached Rob I sat in front of him, as I was supposed to do. He then instructed me to do a proper finish, which was to heel round his back and sit at his left side. Done.

Our trainer told us we would get our results via email within the week. He also said that if we passed admirably, we would be invited to do the silver award. I raised my eyebrows at this; I didn't know if it was better to pass or fail. Whatever happened I would be destined for more obedience training. Repeating the course if I failed and extension skills if I passed. Whoopee. This was the stuff nightmares were made of and I felt like I was on one of these hamster's wheels that had no beginning and no end.

It was a few days later that Rob received notification of my passing. He was elated. I had been summoned to attend for the Silver Kennel Club obedience award. Surreal. This started next week. Talk about hot on the heels of the previously acrid course; how much more could a pooch take? I put my paws together in prayer and hoped that this would at least challenge my thought processes and ask a little more of the grey matter. Any matter for that fact.

j s carle

I won't bore you with the detail of the training I had to go through to achieve this award, which I did, paws down so to speak. The same faces, owners and scathing canines tipped up to this, wait for it, nine week course. The worst part about the training was the section on leaving food if it was lying on the ground in front of you, or not hassling the trainer when he ate a bag of crisps right in your face. As long as he ate cheese and onion flavoured ones he would be fine as I didn't like the smell they left on your breath afterwards as no one wanted to speak to you. I had sampled vinegar ones too but they were too acidic for me and stung my tongue, making me feel like fireworks were exploding on it. Plain were exactly as printed on the packet, plain. I didn't like anything plain. I quite liked tomato sauce ones but prawn cocktail always repeated on me, making me burp profusely - as did gammon ones - as you will know from my Yellowcraigs trip. As for not touching food lying on the ground, that was a difficult one for any Labrador. Of course I could do this with my lead on as Rob just hauled me off it.

One night they had laid out some lumps of tempting cheese on the ground and made us all walk past them without sniffing or eating them. This was a huge ask as for some reason all dogs seem to just love cheese. Probably because it smells like our paws and we like licking them. For me, it also smells like Rob's cheesy socks that I steal, chew and sometimes, by accident, eat. Anyway, to get back to my story: my friend, Mickey, aptly named after a mouse, really toiled with this exercise; the rest of us managed under duress. With us all having successfully carried out the cheese

a lab report

bypass and navigated all the juicy looking pieces, we stopped for some praise by our owners. After some 'good girl' comments and pats on the head, Rob nudged me to draw my attention to the lady in front of us, with the Tibetan Terrier, who was fishing in her pocket and slipping her dog a bit of cheese. I actually felt my head shaking in disapproval. When I looked up at Rob, I could tell he was unimpressed by her behaviour too. What was she teaching her dog? I took my training seriously enough not to condone this type of behaviour and the giving of mixed messages. I should have dobbed her in to one of the trainers but that would have been petty. It wasn't the dog's fault after all - it rarely was. You just can't get the owners these days!

I had made good progress with my down stay and recalls since my Bronze award as I was forced to practise them every night for my supper time biscuits. I didn't mind so much doing this as at least there was an extrinsic reward. I wasn't in to this psychology-type talk about doing something for intrinsic value. I am a dog. Everything is food driven.

The test night saw the same examiner return to check out my progress. He was super impressed with what he observed and how I performed to the best of my ability for at all tasks, so I got the equivalent of an extinction. I mean an exception. No, a distinction. I knew I'd finally get the right term. I was awarded my rosette there and then, sniffed my pals goodbye - adios amigos - and left the hairy little hall forever. It was such a shame our club did not offer the Gold award. I would have been so keen to pursue it, cough, cough.

12

Application of my Obedience Training

You will not be surprised to hear that, in the widest sense, my obedience training was not having the desired impact on my behaviour in, around and out-with the home, that it was expected to have. Disappointing for Rob and Amy, much less so for me.

By nature I am rambunctious and my true personality will always shine through; I would not become a clone or stereotype, as happens when trainers or teachers try to stamp their authority on classes.

Let me offer you an insight to my levels of disobedience. These events I am about to relay are not fabrications of the truth; they really happened. Let's face it - you don't stop

a lab report

living your life and being true to yourself just because you go to classes and become a bit more educated. It is what you do with that new found knowledge that matters. That can be as contrived as you want it to be, as I have proved with the following events.

One night, whilst watching the television, Rob had bought a plush new mobile phone so was in the middle of changing over the SIM card from his old phone to the new one when Amy called him through to the dining room for dinner. Lo and behold, when he returned to his phone afterwards, which was resting on the arm of the chair, the SIM was missing. I watched him frantically turn over the settee cushions, search under and between the chairs, never once asking me if I had seen it, eaten it, played with it, lost it. He really thought, because the card was so minute, it was just lost. Amy, however, was more sceptical. If only he'd chosen to ring the phone I would have been quite happy to accept his incoming call and I might even have vibrated.

The crux of the matter came to light the next day when I was outed. As Amy stood over me in the field as I pooped, she saw this small glistening red SIM card, with its small gold bar code, appear as if by magic. At this point, I didn't have a paw to stand on in terms of denying my part in thieving it. Carefully, with a tissue, she did her best to salvage the remnants of it to show Rob. Needless to say he didn't want the leftovers; unlike me, who always gratefully accepted these.

Keen to get his new phone up and running, Rob enlisted Amy's support by asking her to visit the local mobile phone store in Edinburgh to purchase a replacement SIM card. I heard her regaling the story to him later on that evening about how she had come clean to the man at the counter about how it had gone missing. As she was too embarrassed to speak out with the long line of people listening behind her in the queue, she found herself whispering to the sales assistant,

"You know how people claim their puppy has eaten their SIM card or phone. Well, I am living proof of the phone card."

The man had smiled at her and professed to be a dog lover himself, which was just as well. He then asked if I was a Labrador as he said we were notorious for eating everything and sundry. What was sundry? I had never tasted that. The man had been sympathetic to Amy's cause, finding it rather amusing, so had replaced it free of charge, whilst even retaining Rob's original number for him. She had the gift of the gab just like me I thought, and with what I am sure, a little flutter of her eyelashes, had won the salesman over.

Most days I continued to steal socks and most recently, I consumed one of Amy's sports anklets which she wore with her running trainers. I had stolen it off the downstairs pulley when she had lowered it to hang up the newly washed clothes. It was a mistake really as it had just slipped over my gullet when I was tossing it around and as I can't speak human English, there was no way of owning up. She hunted high and low to find the matching one but no joy. She had commented to me,

"That's strange. I seem to have mislaid a sock Rosie. Hopefully it will turn up somewhere."

Turn up it did. Three days later she located it outside the

a lab report

living room door, a grubby brown colour, after being through a washing machine cycle in my tummy for that time and then regurgitated by me. Undeterred by its colour, being her favourite sock, even knowing full well where it had been for the last few days, she stuck it through a sixty degree wash and donned it again for her next run. As you can tell, money was an object in our household and everything was recycled!

I continued to pinch loo rolls if the bathroom door was left ajar. I'd take them out to the garden and run a white path through the trees and bushes, decorating them in different patterns. The extent of my artistic prowess was equated directly to the amount of toilet paper left on the roll.

I stole shoes and chewed them up; each shoe always belonged to a different pair. I was merely encouraging Amy to adopt a mix and match approach to her footwear. I also stole Amy's glasses, not that they were of any use to me with my eighty/eighty vision.

I chomped holes out of sweaters, which went unnoticed by Rob, who then wore them to his work, until one of his colleagues had passed comment on his professional dress code one day, unaware that the reference had been directly related to the gaping hole under his armpit. It wasn't until he went to scratch an itch later on he felt the cotton of his shirt being pulled through his jumper and realised what the earlier comment had been alluding to. He was not best impressed by me that evening as another sweater was binned. I was ending up a very expensive purchase in one way or another. I am, as they say, high maintenance. As the puppy books say, if you don't want it ruined, leave it out of harm's way. Not that I am called Harm of course.

Undoubtedly, or perhaps I should say probably, although I will leave you to be the judge of this, the worst I did, was to chew a massive hole, well, basically eat, Rob's passport the night before he was due to fly off to Rome on business for two weeks. It was 'Arrivederci Roma' and 'Ciao Bristol', where he was sent instead for two days. Although Rob said the Clifton Suspension Bridge had been structurally interesting it didn't quite match the historic prominence of the Trevi Fountain, St Peter's Basilica or the Vatican. Si! Secretly I think Amy was quite pleased that he couldn't go. Maybe he would get another opportunity at some point when his new passport came through - as long as he stored it in a safe place, that was!

One morning, not long after the passport fiasco, Rob had propped his briefcase up against the bottom of the stairs whilst he nipped to the bathroom before he headed off to work. In his ignorance, and not having learnt his lesson from previous events, he placed a pint of semi-skimmed milk, in a plastic carton, alongside it. The temptation was so overwhelming, that in his absence, I took the opportunity to remove it to a safer place. After heading upstairs to the spare bedroom, carton firmly secured in my mouth, I pounced straight on to the double bed. Here I was afforded a safe haven to experiment with different ways of trying to acquire its contents. Time was of a premium however so I had to be super quick in doing so.

After tossing it around for a bit nothing seemed to have

a lab report

leaked out. More drastic action was needed so similar to my actions of sticking my teeth in to a stolen child's plastic beach ball, I sank them firmly in to the green lid and managed to penetrate it. With this piercing came the delightful sound of escaping air signifying the seal was now broken and the milk was ready for my consumption. Synonymous with my triumph was the sound of Rob returning to the kitchen to collect the usual two dog treats for us, out of our feeding cupboard, as he always did before he left. I heard him giving Coco her biscuit and asking her where I had vanished to.

    His footsteps were ascending the stairs and I heard him returning to his and Amy's bedroom and asking her if she had seen me or if I was hiding under the covers. Now there was an idea I hadn't considered! She mumbled sleepily that she hadn't caught sight nor sound of me. He then peered in the spare bedroom's door and that was when he caught me red handed, in all my glory, glugging back the milk from the moderately large hole I'd made in the lid. My head tilted back down, teeth still wrapped around the carton as milk dripped from my jowls. Our eyes met momentarily before I sprang up on to all fours and retreated to the back of the bed. With the look of outrage, or was it pure rage, he moved towards me with great pace, swiping at me with both hands, trying to snatch his milk back from my gob but I was much too quick off the mark - this was far too tasty to give up without a fight.

    After a few minutes of careering round the room being chased, ducking and diving, jumping on and off the bed and running under it when he tried to climb over it to grab me, he eventually caught up with me and the concertinaed milk carton was prised from my mouth. He then raced back downstairs with it, emptied what little contents there was left down the kitchen sink, and then I heard him fling the carton in to the recycling can. When he returned to the bedroom, I was busy licking up the dribbles on the bed cover, being keen to help out with cleaning up my mess. Mid lick, I was rudely turfed off the bed as he proceeded to remove the duvet cover, before retreating back downstairs again and throwing it in to the laundry basket in the basement. I had started to follow him but instead decided to stay at the top of the stairs and observe him through the banisters - it gave me that relative feeling of safety from a distance.

Without a bye or leave, and no biscuit for me, I saw Rob whisk up his briefcase and depart the premises. No "love you all" this morning! I guess I was supposed to feel guilty for the chaos I had created; making him run late for work and not supplying the office milk but, if the truth be told, I didn't even feel the tiniest bit of remorse. I was the dog who got the milk as opposed to the cat who got the cream. It had been there for the taking and take it I did.

I continued to steal hats, gloves and handbags as part of my everyday amusement. As I was now growing taller I was able to reach food on counter tops (the roast chicken had been particularly delicious - I knew to avoid stealing cheese if there was ever any left out). Beyond that, if I could reach the goods, my mouth would be round them and I was off with my finds. I was always up for a chase, inciting them as often as I could. Initially after learning the phrase 'leave it' at my Silver obedience training, I would often trade my item in exchange for a treat. As I became more savvy and conscious of this game of strategy, I learned to weigh up the

a lab report

worthiness of the swap. Often the treat being offered did not merit me forfeiting my prized possession. I had learned the act of being discerning too. That way I was in total control of the destiny of my goods, and failing all, a good chase around the room or house until I was eventually trapped. That's when I discovered the properties of beds as hideouts. Neither Amy nor Rob were agile, or slim enough, to get far enough under them to be able to haul me out. They used to peer under the bed calling my name and I would give them the beady eyes back from the furthest corner. I'd wave the object around in my mouth, ensuring more damage to it, along with some added slavers for good effect. Eventually they learned pursuing me was a waste of time and energy. Once they were offski, I'd scuffle from under the bed and race after them to taunt them again, rekindling the game. It was only once I decided enough was enough that the game was over. All games were played on my terms. I am a control freak. No, not a freak. I am dominant. I am top dog; leader of the pack.

I am sure I could recite many more of my escapades but I imagine you have managed to note that one of the themes of my book is that I am an out and out thief. I can't help it you see. People present me with options and I am not strong enough yet to reject them. Quite when that day will come I cannot predict so, in the meantime, I will just go with the flow. Maybe I will have to go in to rehab at a later stage in my life to help me manage my Kleptomaniacism. In theory, as it is an officially recognised problem, that gets me off the hook, doesn't it?

j s carle

13

Visitors from Abroad

My first Christmas was made Supercalifragilistic-expialidocious by the arrival of my human cousins from Down Under. I was now nine months old or, in human years, around six; exactly the same age as my middle cousin, Steven. Then there was Daniel, who was nine and a wee toe-rag called Megan. It sounded like a great combination for the fun packed Christmas weekend they were staying with us before heading off to their other rellies up in the north of Scotland.

Their arrival was like a force ten typhoon. Very similar to a normal day of Scottish weather; I was used to a turbulent time, often experiencing all four seasons in one day (not that I would

a lab report

ever experience the fifth type of season now I had been dressed). I wondered how Bubby, now fourteen years old, would cope with all these little people milling around her as she had been in a steep decline of late and was visibly slower in her approach to life; she rarely stuck her head past the back garden, which was only used for her to complete her ablutions. The last time she had ventured out to the field beside us, I had charged off like a member of the light brigade to see my collie boyfriend, Rufus, and Bubby had decided to follow, forgetting her fragility and how weak her poor legs were these days (about time they invented mobility scooters for us pooches). She was almost half way racing over to flirt with Rufus (she did like the boys did Bubby) when she collapsed in a heap. Amy had raced over to her and held her close as she gasped for air and lay motionless on her side. I ditched Rufus in a nano-second and ran over to my sister's side and started to lick her face. I loved her dearly and hoped my kiss of life would bring her back to the land of the living dogs. It worked on this occasion and once she could stand, Amy headed back to the house with Bubby, and me and Coco continued our walk with Rob.

Following this episode Bubby had been making frequent visits to the vet and had recently returned with some special dietary food that tasted worse than a sheep's poops or dried cow dung that had been festering for six months. Boke! It stuck to your teeth, tongue and the roof of your mouth and when I finally managed to produce enough juices to swallow it over, it felt like trying to eat a Brillo pad as it bumped off the side of my oesophagus and burned a hole in my stomach. No wonder I suffered from haemorrhoids as I tried to give birth to what felt like a hedgehog the following morning.

How did I know how Bubby's special food tasted I hear you ask? When Bubby turned her nose up at it time and time again Amy had phoned the vet to find out what she could feed her next. I had listened acutely to the conversation and managed to extract from the dialogue that me and Coco could be given a little in our food so as it wouldn't go to waste given its expense - what did I say earlier about recycling in this household. Not only was I the universal receiver of hand me down beds, collars and toys, but now food had been added food to that repertoire. If Amy thought I was going to eat this horrendous stuff she had another think coming and I made my viewpoint evident on the second offering of it in my dish. I placed one paw firmly on the edge of my dish and flipped it up so it landed food side down on the floor. I then scraped all my Beta Puppy gold food out with my left paw (it is a known fact left handers are brighter) and ate all of this, leaving the gunk behind. Now if that wasn't in-your-face obvious I don't know what was. Point blatantly made! Greedy Coco made no such stance however and gobbled hers down without it barely touching her lips. This is where the breed line is most obvious. I like caviar, or the finer things in life whereas she likes, well, sheep pearls. And what was Bubby being fed instead of her special diet? Gourmet dinners! Amy and Rob had spent mega bucks at the local farm shop and supermarket purchasing steak pies, roast chicken and roast beef, never uttering a word to anyone that their finest produce was going on their poorly dog. The vet had said to feed Bubby on whatever she

a lab report

would eat; I wondered what diagnosis dictated 'feed dog on haute cuisine'. However, the upside was that once I had refused to eat the sickly food I also became the proud diner of steak pie and roast beef as an addition to my Beta Puppy instead of the usual tuna! Yuck had now turned to YUM!! It was amazing to note how Bubby's appetite had increased dramatically in line with the new offerings. She knew a good thing when she had stumbled upon it and was a dog after my own heart. Who said you can't teach an old dog new tricks and what we dogs learn can't be turned in our favour? I like to believe that months of observing me in action had taught Bubby the art of human manipulation and not to settle for anything but the best.

Anyhow to get back to my human cousins. Megan took an instant shine to me - well, didn't everyone fall in love with me at first sight? However she had a magnetic connection with Brambles when she was introduced to her by Amy and Rob and was told she was very ill. It was gushingly sickening to watch her lavish all her attention on her. To suggest I was jealous would be puerile. Megan would lie alongside Bubby's bed, stroking her coat and talking to her like some long lost buddy. On a few occasions she would physically squeeze herself in beside her, cuddle her gently and tell her a bedtime story. They'd then fall fast asleep, entwined together, with bouts of snoring from both emanating from the bed. It highlighted the immense bond between man and dog and evoked the need for every child to have a dog and every dog to own a child.

Leaving Megan cosied up with Brambles, Amy encouraged the rest of us to head out to the front garden to play some footie to run off the boys' energy. Even though it was notably cold for the boys from the Outback, they seemed cosy enough in their knitted grey skull and cross bones jumpers, which apparently glowed in the dark. I like bones so would know where to find them on sun down should I fancy an extra something to nibble on. I wasn't sure what wool bones would taste like but was always game to try out something new.

Once outside in the garden Steven and Dan started to have a kick around with the football. Me and Cokes (another of my names for Coco) joined in so it ended up as a two on two game. I was ubiquitous on the pitch and so multi-talented that I was able to effectively play the roles of attacker, midfielder and defender all rolled in to one. I drew the line at playing the goalie as I didn't wish my face rearranged as the ball struck it hard. That would be Coco's job as it wouldn't make a significant difference to her looks should the inevitable happen.

The ball was rolled in from the side by Rob and the match commenced. Coco sped up the side lines, dribbling the ball from left to right paw, with the odd nose nudge as she went. Her tongue hung out the side of her mouth to help her concentration level, with the odd loose slaver falling on the ball to make it even dribblier. Coco was nimble with the ball and we always joked with her that she could play professionally for Rangers (me and Rob are both Heart of Midlothian fans). Dan ran in towards her for a full on tackle but Coco managed to divert the ball over to me after she heard me bark the word 'switch'. Rob played five-a-sides at work so he had coached us well in the drills and the technical terms of the game. I managed to secure the ball up the left wing. I

a lab report

then flicked the ball with my rear left paw and nutmegged Steven (played it through his legs for you non footie fans) as he came in to try and tackle me. As there are not enough superlatives to describe my outstanding ability I will move on swiftly and continue commentating on the game - Dan was now closing me down so I held up play by standing over the ball with my whole body and moving round it quickly to prevent him getting his foot in to it. Rob was now laughing his head off at the side and Dan was getting highly irritated at not being able to reach it.

Suddenly, I flicked the ball high in the air and booted it with my rear right paw, sky-high over towards Coco. She headed it down to the ground, trapped it with her front right paw and blootered it in to the back of the net past Steven. We were one nil up! Like a loony I raced over to Coco and after a few high fives, we rolled around on the ground in celebration of our stunning goal. Dan and Steven were less than impressed being beaten by not only two girlie dogs but ones who were also much younger at the tender ages of nine months and five years old.

Things had now reached fever pitch as Dan and Steven tried to even things up. The pace was intense as they worked effectively as a team (how good am I at commentating) to dribble the ball down towards our end of the pitch. I have to remark that their dribbling skills were as good as Coco's when waiting to be fed i.e. only superficial and most could see past them! We had decided to play a sweeping back so Coco positioned herself in front of the goal area and made a Scooby Doo wide position, baring all and waving her paws around at the same time. Steven crossed the ball over to

Daniel who did a quick fake and drive to try and take the ball past me: a move often executed by us dogs to an even higher level than those carried out by the Harlem Globe Trotters, but I had him sussed and got down low, used my body weight, of which I had plenty as Tubby Tub, and fell hopelessly on top of the ball.

Dan appealed to Rob as the referee for a penalty, which he was awarded. Coco put her goalie's gloves on and stretched out across our goal mouth and recruited the support of our most avid supporter and coach, Vinnie Van Patch, to give her advice on how to best position herself in readiness for the big take. He had an eye, and an ear, for such decisions. Dan lined up to take the penalty and ran hard at the ball, kicking it firmly and ferociously straight at Coco, who was tremendous in deflecting it as she spun round quickly and it rebounded off her bum cheeks and went over the cross bar. Steven jumped up and down in disbelief.

No time to waste as the ball was now back in play again so I chased it down. I sank my teeth in to it to stop it rolling away from me and at the same time heard a high pitch squealing sound - the ball instantly deflated by about two thirds in size in my mouth. They had handball, football and I had now invented mouthball.

"Unreal" shouted Dan. "She's burst the ball. What a cheat. Game's a bogey."

I knew bogeys as the things that ran down children's noses before they had the chance to lick them off with the tips of their tongue or alternatively wipe them on their sleeve so they formed a green encrusted streak. So, why was our game a bogey? Had

a lab report

it been all green and slimy or would it be replayed at a later stage when we had a new size five match ball?

After apologising to the boys for not having a spare football as such, Rob suggested they could substitute it for one of my large, furry, multi-coloured, stuffing filled balls. A true match ball. They both reneged on this kind offer. It wouldn't have been fair to have played with this anyway as it would have been a home advantage. We could even play with a tennis ball as we were equally adept at dribbling, catching and nosing it. I could even eat it so it looked like an Adam's apple in my throat, which may amuse our opponents. No doubt they would appeal to the referee again saying I was cheating. As if I would be such a low life to try to beat my opponents that way.

In the meantime Rob offered the boys use of our swing ball. This cheered them up no end and suitably suited and booted, they headed round to the back garden to play. Megan had now joined me, Rob and Coco to watch on the side lines, leaving Brambles and Amy, in peace, back in the warmth of the house. Dozy Daniel started off by hitting the ball to Steven, who batted it back. This went on, back and fore, left then right, back and fore, left and right, until I was almost dizzy with watching and just about keeled over. Not long after Steven got fed up being beaten by Dan and wandered off. Megan then took up the reins, but given she was so much younger than Dan, had the coordination of an octopus with eight left tentacles which all wanted to do different things, she proved little challenge to him. Seconds later the bat had been ditched and Dan was playing solo. I watched for a minute or two before moving in closer and sitting underneath the action. Once I had mastered the timing, I would spring up and catch the ball in my mouth, playing ball girl like I saw on the TV during the summer months at the Wimbledon Championships. At first Dan thought this amusing but when he realised I was better than him, as I got to the ball more often than he did, he got moody, flung the bat down and stormed off. There I was, left with a slaver ridden ball and no partner. So much for love all! I know you are supposed to let kids win games but when I was only a mere youngster myself how could I honour this?

Once we were all back indoors the kids put on some music and started dancing around the living room like headless chickens. I tried to join in by jumping up at their sides and gripping on to them; they would take hold of my front paws and swing them back and fore in time to the beat as they pulled me around the floor on my rear legs. Amy joined in and so did Bubby, who just loved to strut her stuff and could always muster the energy to dance, even though she was ill. She was pretty good at it too and stepped in time to the rhythm of the music and spun round and round in circles with Amy. It looked like a mix of a Rumba and Quick Step. She was a real doggy disco diva.

After all the frivolities we were given five minutes to calm down and then the kids were given the task of feeding us. Dan was allocated to Coco; Megan was given Brambles, who required hand feeding of her chicken or beef (sounded like standard issue on any economy airline seat at meal times, 'Chicken or Beef madam?') and I was hooked up with Steven. They made up our dinners and then

a lab report

got us all to sit in front of them before putting our dishes down to let us start.

Once my dish was placed on the floor Steven sat down on the floor next to me to watch me eat. Just as well I wasn't the self-conscious type as I had never been watched at such close range and lesser mortals would have been seriously put off. Me, I could eat my food in front of a pride of starving lions and not be put off one iota; well maybe a slight exaggeration. I might have been put off a little 'ole teansy weansy bit! However, with every mouthful I took being super-analysed, I did my best to eat as neatly as possible and not spill anything on the floor or down my chin. As forward planning was important in life I also ate at break neck speed to ensure that I would have sufficient time left to head over to Megan and half inch some of the roast chicken she was feeding Brambles before it was all gone. I figured given Megan and the crew didn't have dogs, it would taken them a few days to clue in to my alluring ways and suss out that my loving up act was merely a ploy to secure more food. I would do just about anything for food!

Having gobbled my food down, licked out the plate until it shone like a star in the sky, I moved swiftly over towards Megan. She was just slipping me a bit of the roast chicken when Rob came marching in to the kitchen and snatched it from my grasp.

"The chicken and beef is only for Brambles as she can't have normal dog food due to her kidney problem," Rob stressed to Megan.

"Oh," she said in her Aussie accent. "Not even a little bit?"

"No, not even a crumb," he told her. "Don't be fooled by

these pleading little eyes. She's at it and she knows fine well she's not supposed to get any."

Grumph! Bubby smiled at me in that superior way and then turned to Megan to slowly extract her next chicken piece from her hand. She sooked it up in to her mouth like a piece of spaghetti and chewed it for some time to heighten my awareness of its juiciness and make my slavers so profuse that I formed a puddle in front of me big enough to skate on if it had frozen. Steven and Dan pointed to the floor and screeched,

"Look at the Sheila's slavers!"

I tried to do a spaghetti action with the two left hanging, trying to visualise them as my piece of chicken that hadn't been, and after they had slapped off my face a number of times on the way up, managed to get most of them back in to my mouth minus a bit that now stuck to my chin, which I quickly rubbed off with my left paw. Sometimes I did let myself slip a bit and slavering was not very fashionable amongst good looking dams. I would not be referred to again as a Sheila. My name is Rosie!

After our dinner came the opportunity for desert, or did I mean dessert? Let's call it pudding for simplicity as I can definitely spell that! With three little human mouths to feed dinner time was even better than I imagined (as were breakfast and lunchtimes in the coming few days). By nuzzling the kids hands from under the table I made my presence known and was then gifted little morsels of food by them, which ranged from bacon and egg, toast, meat, potato and three veg. I now had a well-balanced diet alongside my Beta Puppy and tuna with sunflower oil. Of the three most likely to

a lab report

give healthy offerings Megan seemed the best bet as being younger than the other two she seemed to be more picky about her eats, like less and therefore happy to try and get rid of it discretely to me. The first night Amy caught her giving me a handful of mince and both of us got a telling off; me for scrounging and Megan for feeding me at the table.

Following our second row within hours, Amy reminisced by telling Rob a story about when she was young and they used to go to an older Aunt's for dinner and how she always made weird and wonderful things that kids would never eat - like curry. When she used to turn her back from the table or get up to pour the juice or wine, Amy and her sister would use their paper napkins to empty at least half of the food off their plates and in to them. Worse still, they then would implicate their mother in the crime (yes, my human granny) by getting her to store the serviettes in her handbag. When Amy's Aunt returned to the table she would ask Amy and her sister what they were giggling at, to which they would answer, 'nothing', and how the tears would then flow from their eyes as they tried to stifle their laughter and contain themselves. For some reason she never seemed to notice how quickly the food had been consumed in her absence or that the napkins had vanished in to thin air; perhaps she had thought they were so hungry they'd eaten them too! What an awful woman my owner was. How deceitful. Now if I had been there, I could have done the same job as the napkins; just what I was doing now for Megan. Amy obviously didn't realise Megan thought the same of her cooking as she had thought of her Aunt's. That old saying is true; what goes around comes around.

For a dog with ADHD type tendencies, even I was glad to see the kiddie winkles banished off to bed at night to allow me some time to bask on my sheepskin rug in front of the fire without being sat on, having my tail pulled or being poked and prodded by little hands. This full-on admiration was exceptionally tiring every moment of the day and even I needed time to recharge my batteries and get ready for the onslaught of the following day. I needed what they termed 'my beauty sleep'.

a lab report

14

Christmas Eve

Knock, knock, knock on my boudoir door. I glanced sleepily up at the clock; yip, I could tell the time on both analogue and digital clock faces. I made it just after six am, which in my reckoning equated with breakfast time. I did breakfast anytime from five am onwards so it had been a long lie for me. The knocking continued, followed by wee voices asking pleadingly,

"Is Rosie coming out to play?"

Amy said if they gave her and Rob five minutes to get up and dressed I would be ready for action then too. I got up out my bed, yawned and did a massive downward dog like I've seen people attempt in these yoga programmes on the TV that Amy works out to. What human on earth would want to learn or be able to perform such a move unless they wanted to metamorphose into a dog? I racked my brain for other reasons. They didn't eat from bowls on the floor like me, which required the flexibility of morph or bendy Wendy to get down to. The only reason I could think of was to be able to look for and retrieve one of my balls under the settee when it had rolled underneath it by accident. Okay, perhaps the move was a tad useful after all.

Rob was first to climb out of his pit and once he'd done so, he pulled on his fleecy top and proceeded to walk over to the window blinds and pull the cord to raise them up. Smiling gleefully he turned to Amy and announced,

"It's snowing. It really is going to be a white Christmas."

Amy jumped up exuberantly to stare out the window and look at the falling snowflakes and the fast accumulating white mass all over the grass. She exclaimed that the kids and me, aka Rosie, were going to be so excited to see snow for the first time ever. With that, she grabbed her cosy jumper from the top of the chest of drawers, pulled it quickly over her head, thrust on her slippers and yanked the door open, raring to go. The kids, who were hanging around outside the room, all bolted downstairs back to their bedrooms. They still had their jim-jams on and obviously had not spotted the snow outside - whatever snow was. Even if they had, I knew that I was a far bigger attraction than it and I would win hands down any day.

I flew after them, taking the steps about five at a time and clinging to the corners of the staircase as I went. They ran in to one

a lab report

bedroom and all hid under the duvet, calling my name at the top of their voices. I dive-bombed the bed and used my nose to flick my way under the covers to join them. Megan was screaming her lungs off and the noise pierced my hyper sensitive ears so I did my best to stomp a paw over her mouth to quieten her up. Unfortunately that backfired on me as she started to laugh hysterically like a hyena instead. Equally deafening. Kids all seemed to be born with an innately annoying screech and for that reason alone I would be glad to hand them back to my human rellies in a day or two before the decibels caused irreparable damage to my luggles. Having reached tipping point by now, I sat on her, pinning her to the mattress in the same way as I used to pin Coco to the ground when we played horsy, horsy outside. The boys started to laugh at me holding her prisoner under my small but weighty frame. I then flopped like a dead weight on top of her and started licking her face whilst gently covering her mouth with my paws to shut out her calling to Amy for assistance.

"Breakfast," shouted Amy.

I never needed to be called more than once when food was involved. I sprang to all fours instantaneously and bolted through to the kitchen, where Bubby and Coco were already partaking of their goodies; Coco had her usual brown soaked pellets like mine and Bubby was having plain fish, hand fed to her by Rob. It smelt, well, fishy, but looked very tasty. Hopefully she wouldn't eat it all and I would get the leftovers if I took my time eating my Beta Yuppy, I mean Puppy. As variety was the spice of life I felt that everyday should bring a new tasting experience from around the globe and an adventure to make my life memorable or others remember me. I am not talking about notoriety but I think that may have been inevitable with some of the events in my life so far.

Amy then told us all, well I mean us dogs, to go out for a pee and poo and encouraged the kids to come out to the garden too. Why I needed an audience to witness my toileting I did not know. She then led us to the back door - it was unusual to get an Amy escort - opened it wide and that was when I saw something really strange. The green grass was engulfed in a white blanket; the white also coated the branches and leaves. It was everywhere - omnipresent - a bit like me.

The kids pushed out past us, still in their pj's, exclaiming excitedly 'It's snowing'. This was their first sighting of this natural phenomenon coming from Aussie land. Megan held her face up to the sky with her tongue outstretched trying to catch the snowflakes on it. Coco and Bubby dived out in to the sea of white and danced around like buckaroos, the snow and cold titillating their paws. The kids started to chase each other and were throwing white man made tennis balls at one other, which Coco was trying to jump up and catch in her mouth. She looked bemused when she did so and they disintegrated in to nothing on impact. Easily fooled was my Coco.

I felt my bottom being pushed gently with Amy's foot, ushering me out on to the cold, soft, white stuff. As I made contact with it, it felt like someone had stuck my pads on ice cubes. I tried to run to free myself of the icy chill firing up my paws but because I was so little I felt that the snow was swallowing me up with every step I took. My body became immersed in it and it stuck to my

a lab report

fur making me I look like the original snow dog. Tired from my minor bout of exercise, I stopped and sniffed it. It had no scent whatsoever. I had never come across anything that had no aroma. I pressed my nose right on to it this time as I couldn't believe that it didn't exude some type of smell. Still nothing. I used my tongue to lick it. Tasteless as well. Nothing better to do then than give it some of my very own special scent and colour, so I squatted as best as I could, and passed out some warm pee. The white turned to yellow and the stench turned to ammonia. If I stayed out here much longer I would have ammonia too. Or was that pneumonia? Similar. Both made you look off colour.

I sprang on all fours, across the garden to a spot where I could do my number two. As the snow was even deeper here I couldn't assume my normal pooping position, or I would have been sitting on the snow itself, so stood as upright as was physically possible to enable me to complete the task. When I finished I glanced round to see nothing except a hollow brownish coloured area in the snow. I peered down it. The smell was repugnant. The heat from my poopies had melted the top layer of snow and they had been magically flushed away below the surface. Vanishing poopie. How cool! This snow stuff had pretty amazing qualities. My mind began to work overtime - what else could be swallowed up by it leaving no trace? My thoughts were rudely interrupted by Rob calling us,

"Right! All of you in just now. Come and get your breakfast, washed and get some warm clothes on and you can go back out to play when you're appropriately clad. I don't want you catching your death."

What did catching your death mean? Another weirdo human phrase which was meaningless. Why did I have to come in too? I had no need to get washed and had my fur coat already on, as did Coco and Bubby, so why couldn't we stay outside and play by ourselves? Maybe being so little they were scared they would lose me in a snow drift. I knew from my own experience only moments earlier that it was possible for things to go missing in the snow.

Breakfast was eaten, as it indicates, at break neck speed. The kids drank down their hot chocolate as fast as was humanly possible and scoffed their toast with marmite 'love it or loathe it' - me - I loved its beefy taste on the crusts I was fed. I had heard the kids telling each other not to eat the crusts as my human granny had told them some fable that eating them made your hair curl. If they had bothered to think about it for a second I was living testament to the fact that that was a whole load of codswallop as there were no curls in my coat after all they had fed me. Saints preserve us - I wouldn't be eating them if there was even the remotest possibility of turning in to a Labradoodle.

The kids were then ushered to get washed and brush their toothy pegs. They were lightening quick at doing this and even I would require convincing about what they had washed in that timescale. Maybe a freckle. However the kids proclaimed loudly to Amy and Rob that they only needed to wash their faces and 'bits'! Quite similar to me really, although I didn't bother with my face, just other peoples', usually straight after cleaning my bits! On hindsight, it was good the kids didn't bother about being too clean

a lab report

as it would have delayed play further and I was keen to make the most of my first snow day, even with smelly people.

Dressed in their cosiest clothes: fleeces, scarves, hats, gloves, pj's with tracksuit bottoms over them for extra warmth, cosy socks layered with even more of Amy's cosy ones, which were far too big for them all, Wellington Boots, which Amy and Rob had bought them all in preparation for a wintry day or for playing in the puddles, we finally headed out to play in the snow...

Bubby was in her element, and the old bones came alive, behaving like some juvenile delinquent. Much taller than me, the snow only went half way up her black sticks. It would have been greatly appreciated if Eiffel had offered me a ride on her back as, being only a third of an adult size Lab, it came up to my oxsters. No chance of me smelling of BO at least. Coco was dancing round the kids as they worked with Rob, who was showing them how to roll a small snow ball along the ground gently but pressing it firmly down, so it gathered more snow and became a bigger ball. He and Amy said they were going to help them build their first snowman for their mum and dad's return later on that day so they would be really impressed.

Four balls later; one huge ball, one middling ball and one smaller ball. Then there was me, who was having a ball. Rob and Daniel rolled the largest snow ball in to the middle of the garden and then lifted the second biggest up and placed it precariously on top. Finally, they heaved up, with the help of all hands, the smallest of the three balls on to the top layer. It looked like some fancy wedding cake with all its tiers.

"Tada...Now we can start the fun part - decorating your snowman. What would you like to put on it?" asked Rob enthusiastically, wearing a massive grin.

He was like a kid but with a five o'clock shadow. He winked at Amy and she smiled back at him adoringly. For what? Building a snowman! She was so used to teaching children having a big one as her husband didn't seem to bother her one jot. I had to admit that I quite liked the fact that Rob had a spirit of adventure and took great delight in doing childish activities. "It keeps you young," my human granny used to say. Not that I ever saw her out designing her own snow grandpa, who might have kept her young!

The kids followed Rob inside to see what goodies they could find around the house to adorn their snowman. In what seemed like hours later, they returned with a bag laden with a multitude of items. Megan delved in to the bag and extracted a long colourful scarf with every colour of the rainbow on it. ROYGBIV or, Rover Of Yellowcraigs Goes Ballistic In Vets. That's how I had been taught to remember the colours. Red, orange, yellow, green, black, indigo and violet. Blue is not as nice as black so in my rainbow, I had substituted them. I scanned the scarf to check it fitted the bill. Yes, it had black in it so good to wear Mr Snowman. Next out the magic bag came a pair of unmatched gloves. One red woolly one, most obviously Amy's as it looked too girly to be Rob's; the other glove was in a macho black and white leather and looked like it had belonged to some biker. It had been a previous find of mine at the beach one day when I was on one of my walks. Morbid Rob had checked to see there was no hand left in it before he allowed

a lab report

me to play with it. He had a vivid imagination and had obviously spent too much time watching CSI or these murder mystery serials. Perhaps he should have taken more time to reflect on why there was only one glove, not two. Handy thought! I laughed at my own joke. I hated other people who did that but I excused myself for such an annoying habit. I had infinite patience with myself - as we all do.

Rob was now showing the kids how to tie the gloves on to the end of sticks he had broken off the silver birch tree. Megan was then gifted the task of jabbing them in to the side of Flakey, my name for Mr Snowman, so it looked like he had arms. Given Megan was so small in height and couldn't reach up very far to put his arms in, the gloves trailed on the ground and he looked more like a Neanderthal man. Never mind I thought, it made half inching them later much more accessible for me. What's next in the bag of tricks I wondered? Dan reached in and produced a carrot. I scoured nearby and there was no sign of Bugs Bunny or any Welsh rare bits. Bunny rabbits were a dying breed I had heard. Too many of them had mixed their toasties (myxomatosis) instead of sticking to a vegetarian diet. For that reason I think I will stick to just eating crusts.

Steven rammed the carrot on to the middle of the snowman's face to make, what I presume, was a nose. Who in their right mind would want a bright orange hooter? Mind you, looking at what Megan chose to wear, with nothing ever coordinating, there was little hope for Flakey ever looking fashionable. That old fable that a carrot improved your vision was about to be disproved as Megan was now engrossed in pressing on chocolate buttons to his face, making large circles to resemble eyes, finishing with a jelly tot stuck in the middle of both. My pupils enlarged at the sight of Flakey's alluring eyes and they would certainly melt in my mouth later. The final design touches to Flakey's face was Steven's two rows of jelly tots to make lips, and Dan's twig stuck in his mouth to resemble a pipe. A smokin' snowman. How alliterative!

Finally, the kids were given a massive pebble each to stick on as buttons to make his coat. In my estimation Flakey would need to keep that white coat on for his trip, later on, to the hospital to secure medical attention for his failing eyesight, high coloured nose and his inability to converse as he no longer had a mouth. My ability to predict the future with accuracy was frightening.

If things couldn't get worse, Dan stuck his Russian trapper hat on Flakey's head to complete the look. That 'look' was like nothing I had ever witnessed before in my short existence but the kids and Rob were intent on admiring their creative talent, expressing how stunningly handsome their snowman looked. They were delusional. He just needed his arms outstretched to complete the scarecrow look! He was the abominable snowman!

So enamoured were they with their work, they decided to crack on and create a snow dog called 'Snowy'. What a lot of time and thought had gone in to such an original name. I watched intently as they moulded Snowy together using various sizes of snowballs (it was a girl dog like me so no pea sized balls required). The finished body was huge with the head fairly small in comparison. She looked like she had some form of body

a lab report

dysmorphia. It was obviously a dog who ate far too much and exercised far too irregularly. I gorged my face lots too but made sure I got at least a good hour or more of exercise each day, as dictated by the Scottish Dogerment. This ensured I maintained my trim figure and was able to consume anything I wanted, without reason. My human granny was very jealous of me as she said she would put on weight even looking at a chomp. I didn't think that would ever have been a reality as her teeth were like the stars, came out at night and therefore she would have been unable to sustain the intense level of chewing required to work her way through one of my chews. For that reason, maybe she should consider the 'dentastix' diet plan. It would be a bone a fide approach to weight loss.

When Snowy was nearly finished, Amy asked Rob to go in to the house and search for some things to decorate her with. A few minutes later he appeared back again, with, wait for it: one of my old collars in hand. He passed it over to Dan, who, after chiselling some snow away from Snowy's neck, clipped it on so it was a neat fit. What a liberty! There was no way Snowy would be wearing that by morning, third generation collar or not.

Reaching deep in to his pocket, Rob extracted six bone shaped biscuits, all in different colours, and passed these to the kids to let them stick them on to Poochini (my favourite composer). Megan stuck her two on as eyes whilst Steven used one of his to make a mouth and the other to make a nose. Dan pushed one in either side of Snowy's head so she resembled K9 from Dr Who. I waited on Snowy to say, "Yes, master" at which point I would have given her a command. She never did, unfortunately.

It had now started to snow heavily so after Rob had taken a couple of photographs of us all beside Flakey and Snowy, we headed in for some hot drinks and cake by the warmth of the fireside.

Being the smallest of the dogs and needing the most heat, I secured my place right in front of the well-stoked log fire. I sat looking in to the flames and became mesmerised by the shapes they made. I must have been sitting there for all of a few minutes when Amy called my name. I turned round to look at her. She burst out laughing. What a cheek! What was so funny? She called everyone through to look at me. They all laughed. Allegedly, and I use the term loosely, my eyes had swollen with the heat and I looked like a Lemur. I wanted to blurt out, "All the better for seeing you with" but worried that Megan would think I was a wolf. After the hilarity and floor show I was removed some distance from the fire to allow my goggle eyes to return to a normal size. It was important that they were fully functional as I would need my X-ray vision later on for when I visited Flakey at dusk.

It was late afternoon when Amy's sister, Emma, and her hubby, Mike, arrived back after their romantic night away together at Crieff Hydro, and a well needed rest from their adorable little children, who were delighted to see them return and eager to show them their snowman and snow dog. They had brought my human granny, Amy and Emma's mum, with them. I wasn't sure if she had been with them on their smoochy break in the hope of finding her a human grandpa. My mind boggled and wondered if the snowman

a lab report

out the back would fit the bill?

They would all be staying at Chez Rosie Posie for the next two nights before heading up north to Mike's parents to spend some time with them. On arrival Mike went in and out several times to the car, bringing in lots of packages wrapped in brightly coloured paper; some had Santa Claus (another relative of mine, just with claws not paws) on them, some had reindeers and some were, well, just brightly coloured with decorative fancy bows and ribbons. He placed them delicately under my Christmas tree and they engulfed the bottom of it. The tree lights glistened over them and they looked ever so tempting. Pity I was supposed to wait until Christmas Day to see what was inside them! Could I handle the anticipation?

When Mike had finished his unloading, we all headed out to the back garden to view the snow creatures we had all helped design and build earlier on that day. There they were in all their glory. Well, almost. The fact that there were no eyes, nose, mouth, hat or scarf on Flakey did not detract from what had been a magnificent attempt to create the perfect snowman. Snowy still looked dog shaped but his collar and decorative bones had both mysteriously vanished. There was no way on earth I was shouldering the blame for all the missing items. I had only taken back from Snowy what was rightly mine, the collar, and then turned my attention to Flakey's attire. I had been far too busy devouring the chocolate buttons and jelly tots on Flakey and was near finishing them when Coco and Bubby set about dismantling Snowy's ears, nose and eyes. As I would like to say, in my best Latin 'sero venientibus ossa' - those who are late get bones!

j s carle

Although me, Bubby and Coco were present at the viewing of Flakey and Snowy, all eyes turned to me as if I were to blame. Funny how people always thought things were down to me. Admittedly, often they were right. To hide my partial guilt, I bowed my head and avoided making eye contact with anyone. I tilted my head this way and that but still made no guilty plea. At that point I thought it best to cut my losses and make a sharp exit back indoors. Megan chased after me waving her gloves around and then tried to chuck them at me; just as well her aim was as poor as her dress sense. She was shouting some garbled message about me ruining her snowman. I wanted to retort that only non-perishable goods, not foods, should be used to decorate such creatures. How could a puppy not climb up such a feature and eat off a carrot nose, chocolate button eyes, jelly tots (big yum) and steal a woolly hat, scarf and gloves. At least I hadn't eaten the hat, on this occasion, and if they put on the search lights, they would be able to find all the clothing stored in my outside palace. What was their problem? The carrot, jelly tots and chocolate were all replaceable after all - which was what Rob was presently doing. Once finished, he removed his own hat from his head and placed it on Flakey's one. The kids found that hilarious, and the new, improved snowman was renamed Uncle Rob II. Amy pointed out that at least they had the photos Rob had taken earlier of them all with Flakey and Snowy to show everyone back in Australia and that every cloud did have a silver lining in that they now had two Uncle Robs. Where did she get these bizarre human phrases?

a lab report

15

Santa Claus is Coming to Town

That night, when all the humans headed off to the Watch Night service, I took the liberty of investigating the goodies which had been left under the Christmas tree by Mike and my own mum and dad, aka my human parents, Rob and Amy. In order to do this I had to limbo akimbo under the chair Amy had placed in front of the living room door, as the lock was dodgy, and this was supposed to act as a deterrent or barrier to me being able to break in. Coco and Bubby watched me from the safe haven of their beds in the hallway, feigning disinterest. I think they had already worked out better out than in! I had worked out that time was of a premium and I had only a finite amount to break in, do my business - no, not that type - and get out again, leaving no trace of evidence of me ever being there.

I was in. The tree lights were all off but the gifts sparkled in their fancy wrappings under the bright moon which lit up the room. As I had X-ray vision and could see in the pitch black, that was never going to be an issue anyway. As I danced excitedly over towards the presents I noticed something out the corner of my eye, jogging alongside me. I stopped suddenly and so did it. I daren't glance sideways. It seemed to be about the same size and shape as me. I moved again, so did it! I lay down on the floor and so did it. My pulse began to thump in my chest and bounce off my rib cage. Was this the ghost of Christmas past haunting me? Or the ghost of Christmas 'present'? Who or whatever it was, it must have come over from the bark side. Brave up I told myself. Stop being such a wimp. Taking my life in my hands, I sprang on to all fours, pivoted and gave a huge, resounding bark in the ghost's direction. Silence. I then fell to the floor in a fit of the giggles. I had been scared of my own shadow which the moon had cast on the wall as I moved through the room.

It was reassuring to know there was no competition for the gifts, so without hesitation I proceeded to the foot of the tree. My eyes widened at the array set out in front of me; Santa had been so generous towards me for my first Christmas. I reversed back a few steps and took a moment to mull over how I was going to play this. Nothing came to mind, so I just pounced on the nearest parcel and as I extracted it, loads of others came tumbling round about me, knocking me on the head as they fell. It reminded me of when I had watched the world domino challenge when they knock one domino

a lab report

at the start and it has a chain reaction alongside the millions of other dominoes. At least in that nobody gets smacked on the head by a shower of parcels. If dominoes fell on me I would get splattered in dots and I'd end up looking like a Dalmatian. I could then play join the dots on the days I got bored. Now there was a thought; maybe Rob and Amy could buy me one of them next.

I started to use my paws on the wrapping like I was digging a massive hole in the back garden to bury my bones in (may be used to bury me after tonight's events). Once the wrapping was partially peeled back I could read the words electric razor. Not something of much use to me and I wondered if it was for Mike, Rob or my human granny. I'd find out soon enough I am sure, when the cold light of day came. If it was for my human granny, I had speeded up the gift opening for her now her fingers were less nimble, so I am sure she would be chuffed at me helping her.

I tossed this gift aside and started on my second parcel. There was a sweet smell oozing through the wrapping and it certainly smelt more inviting. It was more difficult to rip open speedily as it had lots of corners and I had to use my teeth to good effect to assist me. I must have spent a good five minutes of sheer frustration tearing off the heavily sellotaped wrapping before revealing a box covered with multi-coloured baby figures on it. Although I could smell food, there was no visible signs of it as they were encased inside the box, which was like playing with a Russian doll. I used my teeth like a beaver to gnaw a hole in the box itself to reveal a cellophane packaging beneath it.

"You have to be joking," I said aloud. This was like some

cruel game of pass the parcel which teased you stupid by making you think you were finally going to unveil the prize. It seemed never-ending. I peered in through the clear wrapping and I could spot little jelly babies which smelt delicious. Although totally and utterly exhausted from all my efforts, there was no way I was giving up now as I had just about sealed the deal. Another small tussle with my teeth and the cellophane and the whole contents came spilling out across the floor.

I scanned the brightly coloured sweets and wondered which to try first. I opted for a black one, given that was my favourite colour. Yuck! It tasted of liquorice, which I believe is good for constipation. I thought it would have created it, myself, with such a vulgar taste. I decided that I wouldn't consume any more of this colour; anyway it wasn't right to be a cannibal and eat your own sort! Every other jelly bubby was fair game though and after tasting all the other flavours I was fully satisfied with them all. It was a big box and there must have been about seventy or eighty babies to eat but I managed admirably, followed by a big burp at the end as a sign of appreciation. I had really liked the green ones - they were my favourite. I had watched Rob eating a jelly baby once. He bit off the head first, and then ate the body. Prolonging the death was exceptionally cruel. Me, I ate about five at a time so they had company. Towards the end I ate them one at a time as I began to toil for space in my own jelly belly and was beginning to get a sore jaw with all the chewing I had to do to allow me to swallow them over and to prevent them from sticking to the roof of my mouth.

Now finished, I picked up the box and read its label. It said

a lab report

'free from additives' and only contained 'natural flavourings'. I then read that the sweets were made by Bassetts. It all made sense at that point! I would have to write to these glum looking, lethargic, long eared bores to complain as the lack of hyper-additives was now making me sleepy and unable to pursue my gift unwrapping. That may be fine for a slow going hound but not for a working dog like myself who required energy at the flick of a switch. I turned on to my back, and lay on the ripped up wrapping paper, feeling like a heavily pregnant woman. With all these babies inside me I started to drift off to sleep, surrounded by my uneaten black babies. I wondered if I would suffer from morning sickness tomorrow or just indigestion? I needed to have room for my Christmas turkey after all.

The light flicked on in the living-room and Megan stood aghast at the sight of me, comatose surrounded by gift wrap, which made me look as though I was one of the Christmas parcels. She walked over and sat down beside me and started to eat the black jelly babies off the floor. It was her munching that stirred me, just at the same time as Amy came in to find me trying to perform a sausage roll on to my feet. How did these Dachshunds make it look so easy? Her face look liked a woman scorned and she marched over to me, grabbed me in both hands, and with a BD comment I was banished to the garden. I waddled like a duck over to peer in the blinds at the living room window. I could see Amy down on her knees picking up the surplus black babies, shaking her head as she did so, and placing them back in what was left of the packaging. She then picked up the razor box and tucked it under her arm. Finally, after about fifteen minutes of freezing my tootsies off, Rob was sent to collect and bring me back in.

By that time all the children, the other adults and Bubby and Coco, were all tucked up in their beds. I wandered through to the dining room and found Amy re-wrapping the razor in pink angel paper. It must be for my human granny after all! Neither Amy or Rob spoke to me nor looked my way so I headed up to the bedroom to my bed as Santa would be on his way to fill my stocking soon. I liked stockings as I had eaten one of Amy's once when I found it on her bedroom floor. It slipped over a treat. I passed it the next day, with a little help from Rob who eventually had to pull it out from my bottom using one of my poo bags placed over his hand. This extraction was not a pretty sight.

a lab report

16

Christmas Day

It was just after six am on Christmas morning and I heard little voices resounding from downstairs. The kids were definitely up so I guessed Santa must have been. I scanned round my bedroom and couldn't see any gifts for me. He must have left them downstairs so as not to wake Amy and Rob. I toddled up to the side of their bed, climbed up on the edge and nuzzled at Rob's face until he wakened up. He reached out and grabbed my head in his mammoth hands,

"Merry Christmas Rosie Posie," he said. "How are you feeling this morning, you greedy pup?"

I wanted to tell him my belly felt a trifle bloated but there was no way I would be blurting that out and risk missing out on my Christmas dinner. Amy sat up, smiled at me and said,

"How you've not been as sick as a dog I don't know given the amount of jelly babies you ate last night. They were supposed to be for Mike. How did you get in to the living room?"

"Put a sock in it," I wanted to say but knew I was the expert in that domain. She did go on about such trivial misdoings.

I could hear Coco and Bubby mulling around downstairs, cavorting with the children and I was desperado to join them. My fun was being curtailed by the laziness of my owners. I jumped up on to the bed and danced on top of them both, scratching with my paws at the covers, then attacking their faces by licking them with my raspy tongue and sitting on their faces with my bootie until they could tolerate no more. With the duvet flung back, they were finally up.

Adorning fleecy bathrobes (them, not me) we headed downstairs where lots of hugging and kissing was taking place. My human granny was the first to greet me with a slobbery kiss on my forehead so I returned her gesture with an equally slavery lick straight back on her smackers with the intention of removing that horrendous stay-on lipstick she was intent on wearing for days on end. Who invented such an abhorrent product that defied women across the world to remove it except through intense scrubbing? This was not good for one's lips, which were the source for the intake of all food. I would never wear lipstick. Lipgloss perhaps, as I liked the strawberry flavoured one I had tasted of Amy's once. At least that had a food source as well as making my

a lab report

lips lusciously shiny.

Megan was drowning Bubby in kisses and hugs and Coco was getting a cuddle from Steven. Daniel, now nine, was far too cool to partake of anything which should compromise his growing masculinity so to goad him I bounced up to him and planted a big smackeroo on his face, which he swiped straight off using the back of his hand whilst saying 'yuck'. I barked at him for being so ungrateful and then nipped and licked his bare feet ferociously causing him to giggle. He then tried to use his hands to stop me by pushing my mouth away from his feet because it tickled so much.

Emma and Mike came over to me and shook my paw and wished me a 'Happy Christmas'. I willingly played along with this bizarre ritual wondering when we were going to get torn in to the rest of the gifts underneath the crimbo tree.

Talk about teasing things out. It was the height of cruelty as we were all made to sit down and eat breakfast together as a family prior to any Christmas present unveiling. Me, Coco and Bubby were given a scrap of bacon and a little black pudding (a weird tasting Scottish thing which I believe is a relative of the three legged haggis) as an addendum to our usual breakfast. We wolfed this down and then raced through to the dining room to join the humans. I used my finely honed scranning techniques to lure the kids in to feeding me some scraps. They obliged willingly as I got the vibes they also had sussed the quicker they ate their brekkie the closer they came to the main focus of Christmas Day - opening the pressies.

They didn't seem to like their Scottish fry up so we got the cast offs of bacon, egg, toast and more black pudding - I guessed everyone wanted rid of it. I had not long finished my last mouthful when I passed this huge pump from my rear end, which should have caused an explosion with the force it came out with as well as suffocating everyone with the rancid scent. It certainly made the smell of the fried eggs seem like some expensive perfume. Seconds later, a jabbing pain ripped through my stomach and I felt the need to rush outside immediately.

On reaching the garden I paddled a few steps in the snow, then I let go of a long runny poo, which I believe is called dirrea. This is such a difficult word to spell which also comes with a smell. It came out my bottom with a spluttering motion like the sound of the putt, putt motorbikes you get on the Greek Islands. When finished, I moved away from it and it looked at what I had just done before the snow ate it up. I then felt the urge to go again. I squeezed my buttocks together and seemed to empty all that was left of my stomach contents.

Amy was now standing at my side, for what I thought was to attend to my welfare but instead she muttered something about jelly babies. I would contest that they played any role in how I was feeling as this moment in time and would argue, vociferously, that this was indeed a direct result of eating a fry up. Maybe it was an anaphylactic reaction to the black pudding. I had eaten eggs and bacon before, so ruled these out as possible causes. As long as it wasn't the return of my IBS on Christmas Day for that would be miserable. Having gone twice now, my tummy felt back in shape and I now had plenty space available for my Christmas dinner. I

a lab report

have outstanding resilience; it is a known fact that a dog's recovery is swift from such issues.

"Time to open presents," Mike exclaimed.

Everyone headed in to the living room. We all sat round politely passing out presents to each other from under the tree until everyone had varying size of stacks alongside them. My human granny had quite a lot of presents for an old person and I was intrigued, beyond the angel wrapped razor, what other gifts she was getting. However, now that I had my own pile of gifts stacked up in front of me, I had a vested interest in them first and foremost.

I knew exactly what to do to open my parcels from some previous practice the night before when some jelly babies had been shouting through their box for me to rescue them. I had willingly obliged. This time though was for real as these gifts were mine and only mine. I used my dew claw to rip the wrapping paper back on my first present, to reveal a huge, cuddly monkey, which resembled fat cheeked George. I would call him Better Looking George II. He was mine after all so of course he had to be more handsome than Coco's George, which went without saying really but thought I would say it anyway. I tossed him aside for the meantime to see what else was in the offing.

Rob shouted over at me, "Have you thanked Dan, Steven and Megan for your monkey?"

As I hadn't bothered to read the label on the present, well, what puppy or kid does, I didn't know who had given me it and except for being expected to write a thank you notelet, like every grudging child, I didn't keep tabs in who gave me what. That was the parents' role.

Without a moment to reflect, I tore in to gift number two. Wrapping peeled back, I revealed a massive, soft, multi-coloured squeaky ball. Kind of like the one I had already but less smelling of bad breath.

"That's from your Granny," Amy remarked.

I had got a whiff of lavender right enough. Next. This present was apparently from my Collie pals. Hmm...what did they know about playing with toys? I tried not to get my hopes up too much about this gift as no doubt what amused a Collie dug would not stimulate the mind of a Labrador. After all, they would be happy with a sheep. How predictable as that's what I got. A fleecy sheep. I couldn't wait to round it up in my spare time. Not.

My final present, yes, I had only received four presents for my first Christmas, was from Coco and Bubby (which really meant Rob and Amy as my sisters has no pocket money to splash out on such luxuries - as was evident from their appearance). It was wrapped in Snoopy gift wrap and was in a huge box. I liked Snoopy; he was one of my favourite cartoon characters and for a Beagle, he was ultra-cool, especially when he wore his pilot's helmet.

I did my best to tear off the wrapping round the parcel but failed to make much headway so Rob helped me out. With the entire gift wrap now removed, a huge box was unveiled and Rob peeled back the flaps on its upper side to reveal an Aladdin's cave. I stuck my nose right in and peered to see what was in it; there were treats and more treats, biscuits, bones, pig's ears, dentastix (to

a lab report

be guarded closely from my human granny, Coco and Bubby), a de-stuffed soft toy which looked like a skunk and was supposed to mean it would last longer than the usual hour or two it took me to rip it to shreds. Lastly, there was a furry squeaky mallard duck with which to hone my hunting skills. I may decide to pass this useless training toy on to Coco.

I took all the gifts out the box one at a time and was so overwhelmed with my array I could barely decide which to play with first. So I didn't. I started to eat some of my treats. I was just about to dive in to my second pig's ear, when the treats were whisked away from under my big black nose and taken downstairs to the basement. So much for Christmas being a time for receiving!

"Plenty time to enjoy these, pup. You've got months of eating in these packets."

Cheapskate Rob must have purchased these as presents for me instead of having to buy me treats as part of my upkeep. Don't think I missed a trick - I wasn't brought up the Congo like George in his banana boat. I would also need to ensure that these treats were only fed to me and not shared with Bubby and Coco. I assumed they would have been given their own Christmas stocking with their lions' share.

Looking around, I spotted Coco chewing her way through a plastic bone, bought in a nearby hardware store, and Bubby was gnawing her way through a dentastix. How come they had got to retain their presents? Favouritism I would argue. I decided therefore to chance my luck and meandered over towards their treats, to see if I could snaffle anything given they were totally ensconced in their chews. Not so focused though as I was met by wide, white, smiley grins and deep throat growls by both. Perhaps my luck was not in on this occasion. What was the motto about share and share alike on such special occasions as Christmas Day?

I returned to George II and carried him round the room at the same time as perusing everyone else's gifts. Human granny had smellies, underwear, a cardigan, earrings, three diaries (I guess it was likely now she was getting old she would misplace at least two so spares were always good), face cream and some perfume. Where was her razor? Curiouser and curiouser. Nothing worth stealing from her pile, although the cardigan would be quite cosy in the base of my tartan bed, unless it had acrylic in it as then it sparked in the dark as I moved around and I ended up getting electric shocks. I would have to check the label later on as I would then know the intentions of the gift bearer if it did contain acrylic. Perhaps electric shock treatment for my human granny as a way of keeping her mind sharper and to ensure she didn't lose her diaries, or her mind for that matter. Talking of electric, I had spotted the razor in Mike's heap of goodies. He may be a macho man with the razor but he obviously had a strong feminine side given the pink wrapping.

The kids' parcels looked much more enticing. They had been given a tablet each to play their computer games on. I preferred the other type of tablet that melted in your mouth. Megan had some new stripy, outlandish clothing, which would scream at each other when it adorned her. She did like to stand out from the crowd and was a bit of an exhibitionist. A bit like myself really, but I didn't need to do it in such an offensive way on the eyes.

a lab report

There were no fun toys beside the boys. Do kids not play with good old fashioned action dolls or get footballs these days? How about Rob and Amy? What had they been gifted? Jumpers, jeans, perfume, aftershave, a new woolly hat for Rob (I imagine to replace the one I had wrecked in my bed when only weeks old), underwear and... socks. As you know I have a fetish for socks. I don't know why but every morning they are the first thing I steal when I wake up. It means 'home' to me and the comforting smell of day old, cheesy socks is just the best. I like clean ones too... and even new ones. They all just seem to melt in the mouth.

    I lurched forward and whisked up a three pack of socks in to my mouth and ran off. The cardboard wrapper round them was soon chewed off and dumped and I pelted up the stairs with Rob racing after me, taking the stairs two at a time. I was now standing on the top landing with nowhere to go. I was cornered. His hand was outstretched beckoning me to give them up. No way. I slipped through the middle of his legs and raced back down the stairs, millions at a time. Dan had now joined in the chase and he had shut the dining room door behind me and both he and Rob were trying to cordon me off by squeezing me between them as they walked towards me in a pincer attack. I darted under the table for safety. Seconds later a small body was crawling in beside me and a hand was reaching out to grab hold of my socks. I headed off in the other direction, crawling along on my tummy, keeping low, like I do when I squeeze down a bunny hole. Just as I was about to escape to freedom my tail was grabbed by Rob and I was pulled out, in reverse action, from under the table. Who invented tails? They are such an easy option for humans to use when they are losing the game.

With the chase over, and some mega soggy socks, we headed back to the living-room where Amy was collecting all the redundant wrapping in a big black bin bag in an attempt to make things look tidy again. My remaining toys, or should I say the few things I had been allowed to retain, had been collected in to a neat little bundle in a container at the side of the room for me to play with later on in the day.

"Who's for sledging?" Rob asked, clasping his hands together and rubbing them back and fore. Misers did that with their hands and that had been proven earlier when he had taken my Christmas box off me.

All the kids jumped up and down excitedly at the prospect of fleeing down a mountain side at great speed. I bounced up and down to make sure that I was going to be on board for the trip too.

"Right kids, off you go and get washed and ready and we'll all head off after that," Rob enthused.

"I don't think Mum will want to come so I'll get the meal started and put the turkey on before we go and leave her to keep an eye on it whilst we are all out," Amy suggested as she headed through to the kitchen.

My ears pricked up. Turkey. Yum, yum. I liked birds, even though they were a bit finicky to eat and the feathers a bit prickly to pass the following day, they tasted nice. I bet you didn't think feathers had a taste, but they do - much more than slugs and snails

a lab report

anyway.

I know dogs are not supposed to be in kitchens when food was being prepared but my owners are quite lax about this. I always assisted, Sous Chien, cleaning up the floor and marinating it in my own slavers, keeping it crumb free. This meant that anything that fell on to it from the chopping board was clean enough to snatch up, before I ate it, and add back in to the dish on the stove. We all adhered to the five second rule in our house if it fell on the floor but it rarely got beyond a nano second before I had swallowed it over.

I watched Amy remove the giblets from the inside of Cluckie, by sticking her hand up its derrière. Grosse if you ask me. I had to turn my head away as it was excruciating to watch. I hope she never had to do that to me. Maybe only boy dogs had giblets or bits. In return, Cluckie then got some other stuff, called mealie puddin' or a white pudding for non Scots (from Mike's mum in Aberdeen), stuck back in it. It looked even less appealing to me than the giblets had but admittedly, more edible for humans. Amy then massaged its skin in olive oil, salt and pepper, for good measure, before encasing Cluckie in some silver foil wrapping, like a true Christmas turkey. She then stuck it in a roasting tin in the fiery oven for its long haul. I just hoped with all the cooking time she was affording it that it didn't shrink to nothingness as there was eleven hungry Horraces to feed; Me, Coco, Bubby, five adults and three kids. Not that the wee ones would need big helpings like me.

Apparently there would be pigs in blankets at our Christmas dinner as well. I guess they had to wrap up in coats to keep them cosy over their pink, lightly haired skin. I was so lucky having such a versatile coat that thickened in winter and thinned in summer. A bit like many of these women on diets.

Served on the side would be Brussels Sprouts; what a distance they had travelled to join us. All the way from Germany. Or where was Brussels? Was it Belgium? I still had to cover Europe in my map reading and that wouldn't be until I started my agility classes next year and we would be travelling around the country for me to compete. King Edward would also be making an appearance as he was bringing the roast potatoes. What a high falluting, prestigious dinner this was turning out to be. To top it all there would be bread and cranberry sauce and gravy. Only five or so hours to dinner and the opportunity to work up a decent appetite was about to be bestowed upon me in my sledging outing, when we finally got going.

Amy was last to shower and get ready and as I waited on her getting ready I guarded the cooking bird. The smell radiating from the extractor fans girded my loins and swirled around my heart forcing my juices to flow, causing a small paddling pool on the floor. I had just settled down on my slavers when Amy appeared at my side for a quick peer through the oven glass to check Mr Turkey was cooking comfortably. Looking down at me she said,

"You're one big chancer matey," and as a woman on a mission, marched past me and in to the living room to dish out some instructions to my human granny about what to do in her absence to prepare the rest of the dinner, which seemed to amount to preparing almost everything. Bossy teacher. I was amazed she hadn't written out step by step instructions for her to ensure they were followed in

a lab report

her dictatorial way.

We were all waiting at the door now, dressed in warm clothes and waterproofs and me and Coco wore our special Christmas fur coats. What are these you are wondering? They are the coats we woke up in on Christmas Day of course. A bit like humans wearing their birthday suits, except our coats are multifaceted.

We climbed into the car and headed out sledging to Garleton Hill. Bubby and my human granny were more than happy not to come and stay at home for some well needed respite (and a sleep in front of the fire as old folk do - let's hope she didn't sit too close or her eyes would swell up like mine). We agreed that Emma and Mike would meet us at the Garletons and that the kids would travel with us; they were inseparable from me. They absolutely worshipped the ground I walked on after less than two days. What an influential effect I had on young naive minds.

On arrival at the hills we literally spun in to the car park on the black ice, atop the hard packed snow, made from previous thrill seekers. The kids giggled in the back as it seemed more like being on a fairground ride than in a Volvo 4x4. I wedged myself up against Coco so she took the brunt of being flung in to the side of the boot. She was thicker than me, in all ways, to cope with being jostled.

Rob parked up in some previously dug out tracks, which would make his escape easier later on should the snow start to freeze over or more snow full. This was vital on Christmas Day as my turkey would be basting in the oven and we had all these prestigious guests coming for dinner. It wouldn't do to be late. I hoped the turkey would manage to stretch to a good sized portion for all of us. I didn't mind whether mine was a leg or wing or anything!

Once Mike and Emma had parked alongside us the kids were decanted, along with two surf type sledges, which the Aussies were well used to using on the crest of the waves, and an original Canadian wooden, sit-on sledge, suitable for the older but equally willing participants. This would have to be used by the adults of the party, or Coco, who was now almost forty in human years and would no doubt be having a mid-life crisis soon.

Mike had tucked the two surf boards under his arms and Rob pulled the wooden sledge by the string attached to the front of it. I tried to help by attaching myself to said rope and hauling it this way and that to assist. Rob did little to discourage me, as at least it kept me beside him and stopped me running off, as he hadn't bothered to put me on my lead on this occasion. He had obviously gathered that the impending fun would encourage me to stay close by.

We headed out along the tree-lined car park and up towards the open, snow covered hills. Coco ran ahead with the kids and I just tried to bound through the snow without getting eaten up by it en-route to wherever we were headed. I hoped it wasn't too far as paddling though this white, cold stuff was tiring me out and I hadn't even embarked on the main activity yet. I fancied a shot of bob-sleighing as I had been inspired by watching one of Rob's favourite films 'Cool Runnings' which was about the Jamaican Bobsleigh team who went to the Olympics to compete for the very first time with no experience. We had watched it together numerous times

a lab report

and I always found the same excitement watching it as if it were for the very first time. I held my breath as they went careering round the corners of the icy track, my head moving this way and that and my body swaying back and fore with the action. I was so engrossed one time that Rob had filmed me and then played the recording back to me later on. I kept barking at the dog on the screen as it was so like me it was uncanny. He then asked me,

"Do you want a shot, you daft dug?"

I had done until he had referred to me as daft. However if three black Jamaican men can ride a bobsleigh so can three black Labradors. Today was going to be my opportunity to flaunt my stuff on the sledges. He'd then have to eat humble pie. Talking of pie...

We were now high up on an amazingly long, steepish slope and the kids were all champing at the bit wanting a shot. Amy offered to go on the wooden sledge with Megan as it could sit two. The boys were keen to have a shot on the surf sledges, which apparently went lightning quick down the slope. Mike encouraged them to lie face down on them and use their arms to paddle to start them off down the hill and then to grab hold of the handles at each side of the sled once it had gained a little speed.

"On a count of three," bellowed Mike. "You'll all go together."

"One.........two........three"

I was a bit slow off my mark as I was used to Rob saying 'ready, teddy, go' for me so I hadn't realised that the two instructions were one and the same. I much preferred the 'ready, teddy' version as it hyped me up more.

They were off and Coco and I raced down the hill after them. Steven was nearest to me so I managed to get alongside him and then leap on to his back for a ride down to the bottom. He was using his hands to try and turf me off but was unable to grab hold of me as we whisked along at speed. Suddenly we hit a small mogul and were flung upwards in to the air and off our board, which continued to motor down the hill without us, at an even faster pace. I took the glaring opportunity to pull Steven's hat off his head and run away with it; far away from the grasp of any human being or Coco.

Coco was down at the bottom of the hill now with Amy, Megan and Dan who had all managed to negotiate the course safely and in one piece. Amy was calling my name and encouraging me to bring her the hat I had three quarters stuffed in my mouth. At least I was keeping it warm! Steven was heading down the hill to collect his boogie board and seemed unperturbed by me having it. I saw Coco being slipped a treat by Amy so headed over to within a few metres of her to see if she was willing to offer me a trade in for the hat. She held out a tiny biscuit in her hand and I stared at it with my non-plussed look. No deal. We stood, stalemate for a further minute or two. Every step she advanced towards me, I reversed two more back. Eventually she produced a fully grown dog-sized treat from her pochette and that seemed more affable in terms of giving up the hat, which I didn't really want anyway as the colour orange didn't really suit me; it was too garish and obvious for spotting me when I was up to no good. I was amazed that they hadn't thought of gluing one to my head to keep tabs on me. Before sealing the deal

a lab report

I waited for the treat to be placed a millimetre from my mouth, spat out the hat, grabbed the treat and ran off.

The adults and the kids interspersed their shots down the snowy mountain and me and Cokes took great delight in chasing down after them. Coco joined in with me trying to cadge backies and stealing hats as people fell off at the bottom of the slope. There was one point where I managed to gather a stack of five hats, which I plonked half way up the hillside, and they now resembled a mini version of the leaning tower of Pizza. When Amy or Rob tried to come and steal them back (possession was after all nine tenths of the law) I would protect them like they were my own puppies. At one point, they were so close to pinching them back, I tried to stuff all five in my mouth at the one time, as I have a massive capacity to store, and I ran off with them up the hill, dropping all but one along the way. I had an affinity with that orange hat for some reason.

I was now back at the top of the hill and watched as Coco played the mule for the wooden sledge. The rope was attached by a clip to her collar and she would pull the sledge back up to the top as Rob called her from above. I had to admit it was kinda cool if you had no brains and only brawn. I however, would not be commandeered. She was so accommodating. There was only room for one sickeningly goodie-two-shoes like her in any household leaving space for that naughty but nice dog like me who made life mucho interesting. Coco was their slave. Me, I was their slaverer! I had run so hard and fast a few days earlier that I had produced such frothy slavers around my mouth Rob had actually thought I had been using his Gillette shaving foam. I denied all and asked him to check if his shortage was down to my human granny having a fly use of it.

Knowing my fetish to have a shot of a bobsleigh, Amy and Rob thought it would be ultra-cool to take me a trip down the slope on the surfing sledge, sandwiched between them. There would be no escape for me. Amy sat on first, and then Rob snuggled up close behind her and Mike lifted me on. Tucked in tightly between them, eyes closed, goggles on like Snoopy in his pilot role, we proceeded down the slope at a fair lick after a shove from Mike to get us started. It was a bit harem scarem and I felt the adrenalin rush through my paws, head, neck, ears and everywhere I haven't mentioned. I prised open, a tiny bit, one of my scrunched up eyes to see how far we were from the bottom. Far enough! I squeezed it tightly shut again and pressed my body firmly against Amy's in front of me to shield me from the impact of the jolt when we finally reached the end of this roller coaster ride. In the meantime cries of 'yee ha' were coming from Amy who seemed to be enjoying the ride much more than me.

"I feel the need, I feel the need, for speed," Rob was chanting repeatedly.

"I feel the need, I feel the need to pee," I muttered. A sign that this adrenalin rush was not of a positive nature and unless it ended soon, nature itself would soon take its course.

I felt motionless. I peeked out from behind Amy's back in trepidation that this nightmarish experience was not yet finished. We had stopped moving. The ride was over. Yippee, indeed! Perhaps I would need to rethink my aspirations of being

a lab report

part of the Labrador bobsleigh team. But then again, we would be encased in a proper bobsleigh and I would be driving, so in control, where I was best positioned. This having someone else take the lead just didn't suit my modus operandi.

I bounced off the sledge; I had an image to portray. The kids all gave me a clap. My pheromones, or should I have said negative vibes (I am sure they mean the same) had not given me away and the youngsters were of the belief that I had relished my trip down the hillside. My performance had been simply sensational. What an actress! I was most certainly destined for that career in acting I keep alluding to. Perhaps not in the re-make of Cool Running's though, if it could be helped.

I heard Amy whisper to Rob that we needed to get going soon as she feared if she left my human granny for much longer we might return to more than we bargained for. She was moderately concerned that she would be snoozing by the fire while Rome burned. What had Rome got to do with watching the turkey cooking? Not that Rob could tell us anything about Rome either!

"Right everyone, we're all going to make some snow angels before we leave."

Straight after Amy had made her suggestion, she ran out in to an open space and flopped on to the snow on her back. I raced over to her as I thought she had hurt herself. I tried to give her the kiss of life by placing my floppies on her lips and blowing on them and licking them. She was trying to push me off saying that she was okay and told me to go and do my own doggie angel. She then started opening and shutting her legs, like a pair of scissors; she then outstretched her arms and started waving them up and down at her sides along the top of the snow. I think she was trying to fly or she was having some crazy fit or something. She just looked plain mad to me. Seconds later she stood up, brushing the snow off herself and pointed to where she had been lying.

"That's a snow angel. Go and try making one of your own."

Game to try, everyone found their own snow space and lay down on the ground, mimicking Amy's actions. I put my head on the snow's surface and used my back legs to push me along the top of it for a metre or two before stopping to admire my creation. I was an Impressionist. Not like Rembrandt or Picasso, although equally talented, but more along the lines of these mad artists who dot colours around in ad-hoc ways on a blank canvas and claim it as a work of art. I was claiming my snow swirl was a dog angel. It maybe didn't look like one at first glance but if you had the ability, as I did, to interpret it in an abstract way, it was glaringly obvious. This meant it was of a high calibre as the more obscure a piece was, the more it was deemed worthy of analysing its intricacies to give meaning to its meaninglessness. If you follow me? You would if you were in to art appreciation like moi.

Seven snow angels later and a trudging walk (or grudging one where the kids were concerned) down the thick, energy sapping snow, we were back at the car park with the sledges in tow. Within minutes we were loaded up and in the car heading back home for our long awaited Christmas dinner. I sat bolt upright for the whole five minutes journey time back to the house as my mind was so active preparing my taste buds for the wide and varied tasting experience I

a lab report

was about to marvel in. Coco was lying down sleeping on the cosy rug; having lived through Christmas dinner five times now, she was somewhat less excited than I was. Perhaps she knew something I didn't? She had said something to me earlier in the day about a protocol to follow and I would know what she meant later on.

My human granny was standing in front of the oven when we arrived back at the ranch. She had peeled back the tinfoil to let Roddie Rooster tan a little on top. Was that why Amy had rubbed oil in to his skin to stop him from burning and going red like humans do in the sun and heat? She had also added the King Edward potatoes to the fat round him and had turned them a few times to make sure they were roasting evenly. Finally, she said, she had put the bacon wrapped sausages in to cook in the lower oven, then remarked everything should be ready in about an hour if Amy got on and finished preparing and cooking the vegetables. Amy thanked her for being so helpful.

I wasn't a herbivore, more of a Carnifruitavore, grazing on meaty finds on my walks, brambles (not my sister, I am not a cannibal) on the John Muir walkway, and on the pick-my-own raspberries from the canes in my own garden. Coco was a dab hand at this and I had emulated her technique of pulling them off by pouting my lips over the fruit, then pulling quickly, leaving the cores or husks behind. Voila! I also ate the fallen cherries from our tree, spitting out the stones as they weighed heavy in my tum, tum. I could also dislodge a few of the pears, from our miniature rootstock tree, by thumping my torso off the bottom of it. I had managed to get three so far doing this. Even though the process involved made me a trifle battered and bruised it was worth it as they were really scrummy, wummy. Given the tree only yielded about six pears and I managed to eat fifty percent of them, I was not that popular with my owners. But let's face it - who peared?

I could take or leave veggies; carrots, peas, beans and most definitely, those non reputable, Brussel Sprouts. The one time I had eaten beans they had made my belly really bloated, like Vegans get from eating all these pulses. It culminated in making me pass a lot of very smelly wind, causing Rob to extradite me to the garden for the rest of the evening claiming that he would needed to have had a gas mask fitted if I were to be allowed to remain in the house. Life was so unfair. It was alright for him to fart regularly but the goal posts changed when it was me. His were much more pungent than mine and I never complained about them, well, what dog does as we all lovely highly scented things. What bugged me the most was that he had the audacity to fob his pumps off on me. Rotten so he was, to the core. The smell proved it!

Moving swiftly on to carrots. As you know I had the displeasure of munching one off Snowy's nose yesterday and it hadn't been very appetising so I was more than happy to take a rain check on them, albeit I was developing more of a liking for orange things, in particular, hats.

Although I had never tasted peas before, and I believed they were Mike's favourite veg hence on the menu, their name did nothing to entice me. Who wants to eat green coloured ball shaped things with such a repelling name? That leads me neatly on to my next topic, Brussel Sprouts. The less said the better in fact as to pay

a lab report

any lip service to them gives them more credit and air time than they deserve. I couldn't contemplate why anyone had ever invented such atrocities. I had heard they were barely palatable even smothered in butter, so I would add them to my list of most disliked foods, along with slugs and snails and puppy dog tails. I would be happy to just have the butter alone. I just love... butter. I had eaten a massive tub of it once when Amy had left it on the kitchen worktop when she was entertaining friends for dinner. I had managed to pull the almost full container down on to the floor and carry it to the upstairs landing where I licked my way to heaven. The stain on the carpet from regurgitated, stomach churned butter overnight, allowed to soak in for hours, was not a pretty sight. Nor to think of it was Amy's face the next morning as she scrubbed and scrubbed to clean it up, which took the best part of an hour. Since that time Coco has always jumped over that bit of carpet I sicked up on. Maybe because it is a bit greasy and she may slip?

The kitchen door opened and Rob peered round it to ask Amy how long dinner was going to be as everyone was starving. She retorted that it was nearly ready but she would feed us dogs first to get us out the way. Nice! We were being referred to as pests. I'd remember that.

"Brambles, Coco, Rosie... come and get fed," Amy called in a light-hearted, cheerful tone.

As I was already hovering outside the kitchen door I had already arrived. Coco and Bubby toddled through from the living room, where they had been dozing in front of the log fire. I watched with intent as Amy mixed up the food in our dishes with some cool water from the tap. She then placed them down in front of us and told us to 'go'.

I stared in to my bowl. I then put my nose close in to sniff its contents. There was not a sausage of difference between what we were normally fed and what should have been our 'special' Christmas offerings. It was just an every-day dog's dinner. I was totally flabbergasted. I looked over at Coco who gave me a quick wink and mouthed the word 'protocol' to me, so instead of procrastinating about it, I just tucked in rather than risk my dish being lifted and getting nothing. Bubby, due to her kidney illness, was getting steak pie with some little chopped up sausages in her dish to make it ever so flavoursome. Sometimes I wished that I could be ill too.

The human kind were now gathered at the dining table and were munching their way through the first course of prawn cocktail. Why this was seen as such a traditional starter for a Christmas meal, I don't know, as prawns are scavengers and munch on all the dregs on the sea bed. I felt it was a bit like the pot calling the kettle black when Amy and Rob told me off for eating rubbish yet ate shellfish which did exactly the same, if not worse than me.

I moved timeously between the kitchen and the dining room doors as plates were cleared and then re-stacked with food. I watched 'panefully' at the kitchen door as Rob carved the turkey and dressed the plates with slices of meat, roasted potatoes, pigs in blankets (I had managed to put one and one together after hearing my human granny use the sausages wrapped in bacon synonymously with pigs in blankets and had a scoff to myself when I realised

a lab report

that no pigs were coming to dinner after all), green beans, not the ones that made you pump, carrots and peas. Plates were carried through two at a time until all seven were at the place settings and the door was firmly shut behind, locking us two drooling pooches out. Brambles was back lolling in front of the fire, doing exactly what I would have been doing if I had been fed what she had!

We watched every forkful taken by every member of the table. The carpet below us was now awash with sticky slavers and my Cremola foam, frothy act was up and running again. As the kids' plates had only small amounts on them they had just about eaten every morsel, except for that one token Brussel Sprout that gets placed on every unassuming child's plate in an attempt to coerce them in to trying it. They too could spot and smell a miniature cabbage a mile off and were not fooled into eating it, even though hungry from their day's sledging.

Christmas pudding had been served, with the brandy sauce, even to the kids, encouraging them to sleep well in a few hours when they would head off to bed. I had heard brandy was good for dogs too, especially when walking in the mountains, as the St Bernard carries a barrel of it round his neck to drink when he gets thirsty. I wondered if, after a few mouthfuls of it, it took him longer to navigate his way home along a straight path? Could the police charge a dog under the influence? I liked having all my 'facilities' around me so I would stay off the drink unless required to partake of it for medicinal purposes - a comment I hear many humans making as an excuse for their over-indulgence.

Just as I had decided Lady Luck was not going to shine on

me tonight, Amy called me and Coco in to the kitchen. We sat in perfect tandem at her feet, with elegant poise. One needed to do one's utmost to impress when scrounging. Rob was standing behind her, tearing off little bits of turkey meat from the carcass and putting some in to my pink bowl and some in to Coco's blue one. If that wasn't pleasing enough to the eye, he then added to it a scissored-up sausage in bacon and a small pouring of gravy. My eyes had enlarged to saucer size in anticipation of the meal I was about to gorge myself on. He then dangled a Brussel Sprout over mine and made some off-the-cuff comment to Amy about me being a gut bucket and he could prove it through me eating one of these. Amy told him not to be so cruel, but giggled as she said it. Imagine having a laugh at my expense. Just as well I had broad shoulders and was not easily offended by such poor humour.

Amy put our dishes down on the ground.

"Merry Christmas, honey buns," she grinned. "Let's hope this warms the cockles of your hearts."

I didn't care that the phrase was gobbledygook; all I was interested in was feeding my greedy little face. It was tasty, tasty, very, very tasty. It was very tasty. Although I had finished the contents of the bowl in super-fast time it was still high in turkey and gravy fumes. This tasting experience had been heaven scent and I proceeded to spend time licking round every millimetre of the bowl for fear of leaving any minute bit. After watching me for a few minutes, Amy eventually extracted the bowl from under my nose. I had gulped in so much air as I ate that I burped loudly and forcibly. A true sign of appreciation. I would add this meal to my

a lab report

bucket list of things to repeat before I died. As I was going nowhere fast, this meant that I would try to repeat it as often as I could just incase of an early departure.

Content and full, I made my way through to the hub of the house to lie in front of the fire with Coco and Bubby. Belly upwards to the world, legs splayed and airing all, I fell fast asleep immersing myself in my vivid dreams. Who in their right minds would want to watch Christmas repeats and the worst television of the year when my own entertainment was much superior? They were welcome, of course, to play some bored game like Monopoly - enough to make anyone fall asleep

j s carle

17

Boxing Day

Virtually all the snow had vanished overnight and all that was left of the snowman and his dog was a mushy, slushy mess and Rob's redundant hat on the ground. I picked up his soggy hat and added it to my accumulating pile of jumble which was stashed in my kennel. Once mountainous I would pass all my acquired goods on to sell at the Dog Aid Society, which supported dogs much less fortunate than myself. No one could ever suggest my motives were not for the greater good of others.

Once everyone had been washed, fed (me again for a second time courtesy of under-handedness at the table) it was decided that we would head out to the beach for the morning, without Emma and

a lab report

Mike who would stay at home and pack up everything in readiness for their journey up north to the in-laws later on that day. Bubby looked more than happy to stay at home again with my human granny, to get their three r's. Rest and Relaxation from Rosie.

As you know I just adore the beach in all its manifestations. Perhaps if we were lucky, we would even get an ice cream from the van man. Whoopee or Whippy? The car journey was interesting as the kids bickered with each other in the back. In order to spice things up and add fuel to the brewing storm, I used my paw to tap them on the back of the heads from behind my bars. Obviously they would never have incited me for such a crime and hence blamed each other. This led to World War III breaking out as they hit and poked each other as pay back. Coco shook her head at me in despair of my cheap tricks to provide free entertainment for myself but I thought it was très amusing. She always did walk the higher moral ground and was risk averse. Boring. Me, if the opportunity was there then why not exploit it to the maximum. That way I would live life to the full.

As the car pulled up at the beach car park I pressed my nose against the back windscreen to get a closer look outside and to plan my excursion. I had things to do, places to see and people to meet; this should have read havoc to create, things to steal, rubbish to eat and the odd bit of business to attend to.

After climbing out the car Rob and Amy opened the back doors for the kids to get out. Apparently there was a child lock applied to stop them opening the doors from the inside and launching themselves on to the road as the car was moving, or even better, I mean worse, escaping from the car un-noticed. Great for parents though and we should have taken full benefit from such a marvellous invention and just left them behind and gone for a walk ourselves. After all, little people always made walks much slower as we had to pander to their needs instead of mine.

Rob slung a rucksack on his back which contained some warm drinks, treats for us dogs, a rug, buckets and spades. I wondered what we would be doing with all of these things. Perhaps using the spades to bury the kids - hypothetically speaking of course.

Steven was requesting to walk Coco on her lead and Daniel and Megan were arguing over who was going to walk me. "I don't want to walk either of you," I wanted to say, as you're both too slow for me and I end up having to pull you along which is muchus extra work or me. Much to my dismay Amy told them they could both have a turn of me. Nightmare! Why was I always the dog who was passed from pillar to post? It was difficult always to be rational about my popularity.

The boot was opened and Rob cautiously opened the inside cage, grabbing me quick smart and slipping my rope lead over my head and enticing me down to the ground. Steven was able to put complying Coco's lead on and she jumped down and stood patiently beside him. Amy locked up the car, and after checking that the lead handles were securely wound round the kids' hands, we proceeded to the woods. Normally we would have been released from our nooses but to keep the children happy we were kept on for their sake. Whose walk was this I wondered? Was that a rhetorical

a lab report

question? Me thinks so.

We were well in to our mundane walk through the woods when Megan started whinging that she needed the loo. A 'number one' only she exclaimed! Too much information I thought. Amy inquired if she could hold on until we got back to the toilets at the car park but, of course, she couldn't, so she told Megan to head off the beaten track and go behind one of the big oak trees and just to shake dry as no tissue paper could be used in environmentally friendly places as it wasn't biodegradable. I am sure Megan totally understood this concept. A teacher never failed to be a teacher did they? I was slipped off my lead to chum her. After she had done the deed, I pee'd on top of it to cover her scent. As I was busy doing so she shouted at the top of her voice,

"Rosie's doing a pee on top of where I've just been."

Talk about letting the cat out the bag - metaphorically speaking of course or I would have been chasing after it at this point. I did not like drawing attention to my toileting habits in public places, nor any place for that matter, and her sharing my most private act with the world was quite inappropriate. After shaking my bootie to dry off my drips, I took this opportune moment to slink off.

Dan and Steven were throwing a stick for Coco so I raced over to join in. Being nimble I managed to seize it from Coco's jaws and belt off with it in the opposite direction. Great way to get a chase and it worked a treat. Coco, Steven and Dan were now in hot pursuit of me so, to make it more difficult for them, I headed in to the thick undergrowth. Dan was the first to lose his footing and fall his length. Steven then tripped over him as he was hot on his heels. I stood still watching the drama unfold and did a muffled stick gruff out the space at the side of my cheeks. What a hopeless bunch. This was a walk in the park, or should I say the woods, the competition was so easy to beat. Coco had stopped to check that they were both okay; a dog with empathy. Now wasn't that sweet? I chuckled at the carnage I had created. I was so engrossed I hadn't noticed that Megan had now sneaked up behind me, along with Amy, who had taken a firm grip of my tail and her other hand had grasped my scruff. I was well caught. The lead was looped tightly round my neck. Megan then prised the stick from my mouth and passed it over to Coco, who was still unattached and trusted enough to proceed without being linked up to anyone. She flashed me a winner's grin. Smarmy pooch.

Rob walked slightly ahead of us now, hand in hand with Steven and it looked ever so twee. I felt a wrenching, or was that retching, in my stomach. There was little doubt Rob would make a loving father to some wee tykes. I just wasn't sure I was ready to share him given that this was a near life experience I was getting at this moment in time with the visitation of the gruesome threesome. It really did take the attention off me and that was not good for a pre-pubescent pup. I needed nurturing or I may grow up with behavioural problems due to neglectful parents. I would be diagnosed with ADHD and given tangle-toys to play with to improve my levels of concentration. I liked the sound of that. Anyway, better to have ADHD than OCD as that would hamper me eating any leftovers off the ground as I would be too

a lab report

worried about who had touched them or about washing them first before tucking in. Not good for a Labrador who is the canine gut bucket and takes contributing to a cleaner environment very seriously.

Dan was even further ahead now playing a game of races with Coco, who seemed to be letting him win to boost his ego. I would never have done that as such trickery only leads to problems at a later stage when he wouldn't be able to accept losing. It is one of life's lessons - admittedly one that I am not familiar with, but I am an exception to the rule.

Megan still had me on my lead and walked alongside Amy. The pace was cringingly slow and even the slugs on the path seemed to be moving faster. I had tried a slug once but didn't like their rubbery texture and they tasted yucky. Perhaps if they had been salted first? I was amazed some Michelin chef had not tried to make a fancy dish from them - after all there was now a restaurant chain called Slug and Lettuce. I couldn't imagine that smothering them in lettuce, also tasteless, would make them any more palatable. Yes, 'lettuce' not eat them as they taste so repulsive. Marginally worse than slugs are escargots; the posh name for snails which does nothing to mask their insipid, slimy taste. How they belong to the insect group 'gastropods' I would never know. There was nothing I could stomach about them at all.

It was good my mind was wandering as the speed we were moving at was beginning to work me up in to a state of extreme frustration. There was an inherent danger when I got to this point as it usually meant when I was released I would run around like a possessed loony to free myself of all my pent up energy. A blind eye and a deaf ear also came in to play at this point so if there was any come back for my actions I would plead insanity.

Distraught, broken, demented, actions over took my being. Head down, body low, and without warning, I blasted off at full pace, like a Husky pulling its sled. I raced forward towards Dan and Coco, dragging Megan in my wake. Her little legs were moving at a million to the dozen trying to match my astounding speed. Unable to do so, she released my lead at the same time as falling head long into a muddy ditch which was awash in leaves. Oblivious to this, and enjoying my moment of freedom, I sprinted onwards to Dan, who at the command of Amy, grabbed my lead, bringing me to an abrupt stop. Foiled!

Megan was now moaning about wanting to go home as she was dirty, cold and tired. To brighten up her spirits, Amy gave her a piggy back ride, which was great for all of us as it meant that the speed picked up significantly. Curiously enough, Dan wasn't remotely interested about walking me on my lead now. I wonder why? Was it because he had seen what had happened to Megan or that he couldn't man up to the challenge of my sheer speed and power?

We were now emerging from the woods and had started to head across the grassland to the sand dunes and down on to the beach. Due to a previous misguided walk by Coco back in July, and my unpredictable behaviour in terms of leading my little cousins astray, Rob kept me firmly on my lead to assure me of reaching the beach safely. I had better get off this lead soon or I would be

a lab report

going out on strike and doing a mumping Megan impression. Not that she would see anything of herself portrayed in my dramatic performance. I would lie down and not move from the spot even if they tried pulling me along the beach on it. I would cough, splutter and choke in protest, drawing lots of attention to myself and ensuring all the passers-by could see and hear me. They would tut and shake their heads at my owners as they would be viewed in a bad light. To be honest, they were best viewed in a bad light anyway, as was anyone less attractive than me. Unlike moaning Megan I bet you I wouldn't be given a backie home for my failure to fall in to line or for feigning tiredness. Puppies got tired too. Tired of not getting our own way.

Coco was now sprinting ahead with Dan and Steven and they had disappeared across the top of one of the dunes. Rob began to break in to a jog with me, obviously beginning to panic a little as the children disappeared from sight. Me - I quite liked the fact that they had done a vanishing act. Megan was still bouncing about on Amy's back getting her free gratis piggy back ride. Why they called it a 'piggy back' I would never know as I had not seen any pigs give backies to children. No wonder these colloquialisms confused dogs like me and we got them mixed up when trying to articulate them. None of them made any reasonable sense unless you were deranged yourself.

Rob and I now stood at the top of this massive sand dune, which felt like I was standing on top of the world. Steven and Dan were climbing their way back up to the top of it, huffing and puffing as they did so. With a quick re-assuring pat on the head, my lead was unclipped from my collar, at the same time as Rob asking me to behave myself. Sure!

I ran at twice the speed of light down the dune towards Steven and in my usual uncontrolled fashion, went hammering in to his legs, knocking him flat to the sand. He proceeded to roll, like a sausage dog, down the remaining length of the dune. I ran alongside him, jumping up and down and when he finally stopped, I pounced on him and licked his sandy face. I was aware my behaviour was being unduly observed from the top of the dune by Amy, Rob and Megan. I looked around for Coco, who seemed to be making the most of the opportunity to absent herself from the pack and partake of a swim in the ocean. Hopefully she would be less smelly as the result of this as her feet were extra pungent at the moment with the cold weather and the central heating going full-blast in the house, causing her to sweat profusely through her pads. When she walked on the slate tiles in the kitchen she left sweaty paw marks in her trail. Pretty hoaching if you ask me. That was one of the differences between coming from a privileged background as opposed to a working class background. Gun dogs are smelly creatures whereas we show dogs only ever glow.

Megan wriggled down off Amy's back and asked if she could race down the dune with the best of us. Given my immense strength I was back up to the top of the dune in a jiffy. Dan was now careering down it, his speed out of control, his knees buckling below him and spectacularly somersaulting to the bottom. When he finally came to a standstill I accosted him and bounced all over his body, tugging at his sleeves and trying to nibble his ears. He

a lab report

was trying hard to push me off, and he wouldn't have normally managed, but at that moment in time I had noticed that Megan was now on her way down the steep descent. I pummelled up the sand towards her and latched on to one of her gloves, causing her to try and hold on to it, so we wrestled with it, culminating in me pulling her down to the ground too. She giggled as she continued to roll, like a jammy doughnut, to the bottom, ending up alongside Dan. I used this opportunity to run off towards the sea with her glove, flicking it around ferociously in my mouth so it slapped off my face, making me even more hyper than the presence of a full moon. Why us dogs liked sadomasochism I can't explain, but I know humans found it highly amusing; it gave us the slap they wanted to give us at times for being such toe-rags.

    I was now standing in the sea alongside Coco and the glove hung out of the side of my mouth, just about, but not quite, dangling in the sea water. Rob, Amy, Megan and the boys were now at the water's edge trying to coax me to pass them the glove with the command, 'give it to me'. This evoked no reaction from me whatsoever and I remained just out of reach. Gallous Megan had now taken a few steps towards me in the water, as she had her wellie boots on, until she could go no further as the sea was about to lap over the top of them. I put my paws in to reverse gear and moved a few feet backwards at the same time as a crashing wave hit me hard on my bum cheeks. Brrr... A long stick was then poked in my direction by Rob, who made an embarrassing attempt to hook the glove like I'd seen humans do at FunFairs when they tried to hook a duck in a pond. It just ain't ever going to work with me as

I am not an inanimate object. I moved my head this way and that, up and down, round and round, making grasping the glove nigh on impossible. Even Coco seemed to be prolonging the agony for them as she acted as a further decoy by grabbing Rob's stick and running off with it. Sheer frustration was now taking over and Amy snarled at me, "Leave it." So I did. Right there and then, in the deep blue sea. I then sprinted past them to give chase to Coco with her stick as they stood aghast looking at the fast sinking glove about to make its home on the sea bed. Off with the shoes and socks, and Rob was in to rescue it. He wrung it out, stuck it in his pocket and gave Megan his own cosy gloves. Real future dad material!

All the crew then headed back up towards the dunes to a canopy with a small cavern. Sheltering inside it Rob shoogled off his rucksack, opened it and removed a waterproof rug, which he spread out across the ground. They all sat down and huddled together on it to keep warm. Some brightly coloured plastic cups were then passed out and the kids wrapped their wee hands around them. A red thermos flask appeared and each cup was filled up with some piping hot brown coloured liquid. Dan smacked his lips together as he swallowed it over, remarking how much better hot chocolate always tasted in the cold. Megan and Steven agreed like two old codgers sitting on a park bench passing the time of day. Given my recent behaviour, not that it was teetering on bad or anything, just mildly disobedient, I decided to observe from afar and not test the boundaries. I knew I was still due a row for the glove escapade. Greedy guts Coco was well in on the act though and was getting to lick out the remnants of Megan's cup. I hoped she made a

a lab report

better job than Cold Water.

With the cups and rug repacked in the ruckie, Rob distributed the buckets and spades he had brought along for the kids to create their own sandcastles. Coming from warm climes they knew exactly what to do with these implements and set about building a grand castle and moat down near the sea. They filled their buckets to the brim with sand then poured some sea water in to them, turned them upside down, smacked them on top with their spades, and hey presto, there was a sandcastle. This was the first time I had witnessed the building of houses on a beach and wondered how long they would last when the raging tide came that night or, if three little pigs would come along and huff and puff and blow them all down? I guessed not, as they had all been eaten at our Christmas dinner the previous night.

Dan was now using the spade to dig a moat surrounding the castle battlements to allow the sea to be channelled up towards it and flow round it, preventing it from any invasion. I was a world champion digger of holes, without spades, and would have been quite happy to have used my talents to assist. Nobody ever asked though so I just set about digging my own whole nearby and flicking the sand up over everyone, who moaned about me getting in the way. Amy was therefore charged with walking me and Coco along the beach, as far away as possible, to keep us out of harm's way. Killjoy!

When I returned from my walk, the kids prototype was just about finished and Megan was strategically (perhaps I am being disingenuous) placing some shells around its outside wall. Given I was back on my lead at this point, for less than obvious reasons, I was unable to add some final touches of my own, which would have made it more flamboyant and raised it from basic to Rosieastic as it did lack a certain je ne sais quoi. I was very artistic when I applied myself, reference the Snow Angel.

Once all the finishing touches had been applied, we gathered round to admire its aesthetic value and design qualities. Rob then took the obligatory holiday snaps of what we had got up to on our, I mean their holidays. If any of these photos appeared on Sniffynosebook I would vociferously deny any participation in the poorly constructed Castle Moat. I would tell my friends that it was designed and built by Coco's fair paws. She would never work again - not that she ever had. I was yet to identify Coco's vocation in life. She was good at scrounging. Was that an occupation? Me, I was master of all trades and jack of none.

I had clocked the fact that so far I had not been dished out any of my treats that had been packed in the rucksack. To my knowledge, which was immense, I don't think Coco had been given any of her treats either. My motto was why traipse something along if it wasn't going to be of any use? That wasn't a reference to Megan, though it could have been, it was alluding to my sustenance. How could I be rewarded with some food to keep me going? I would soon be skeletal with all this intense exercise. I racked my brain, which took a whole of two seconds before it spiralled back to the thought of food. I would just need to use any tactic I could to win me a reward.

We were walking along the beach on our way back to

a lab report

the car park when the kids headed off to a rocky outlet to potter about. I joined them and was very charitable by allowing Megan to lean on me, using me as her stabiliser as she crossed from one mossy, seaweed covered rock to another. I had massive feet which resembled a grizzly bear's paws and gripped firmly, like suction pads, to the slippery, lichen covered surfaces. I turned round to double check Amy and Rob were watching me doing my good deed otherwise I would be ditching the Good Samaritan act if it wasn't going to earn me some nosh. This may sound selfish but, let's face it, no-one in their right mind performs these sort of acts for little or no return - do they? Even if they do, I don't.

The boys and Coco were a bit more gung-ho than Megan and were jumping from rock to rock, showing off their inability to realise the inherent danger or jeopardy they were placing themselves in. Perhaps that was my inner jealousy speaking as it looked much more fun than what I was doing but, then again, mine had a purpose.

We were all off the rocks safely now and Amy and Rob had gathered the kids round and given them small handfuls of treats to feed us with. Megan started by feeding Coco some of hers. I wanted to shout, "Oye, you. I am down here. I have just been your faithful dog guard, keeping you safe crossing all these rocks and this is how you repay me - feeding Coco first. Thanks for nowt." If this is what executing a selfless act did for you this would be my first and last.

Just as I was going in the huff, Rob reached down and tickled my head, giving me an extra large biscuit bone as he did so. This was crunched over and swallowed at speed, allowing me to be fed some smaller treats by Dan and Steven. I had gone off mean Megan, who had now finished her bundle of treats, having lavished them all on Coco. This was most definitely the final time I offered her my hand of friendship for it to be bitten off.

Me and Cokes were placed back on our leads and within five minutes walking time, we were back at the car park. Rob flung the rucksack back in the boot and then issued the boys with a towel each to dry us. Dan was given the pleasure of me. I did my best to make this as memorable an experience as possible for him, ranging from me biting and holding the towel with my teeth, playing tug of war with it, and then flopping on my back making it nigh on impossible for him to dry me. He thought my behaviour was funny and ended up just flicking me a few times with the towel and then standing back from me pretending he was going out on strike. I thought that was amusing too. There was no way I was getting back in the car in my sand blasted state so Amy took over, and holding me firmly with her arm placed under my body and through my back legs, she used her free arm to work the towel firmly across my coat, scouring my body. I knew better than to try and mess around with her at the helm as the alternative would be a cold hosing again; to be avoided at all costs.

Dried, back in the boot with the car windows open to give us some fresh air, Rob, Amy and the kids made their way to the ice cream van at the foot of the car park. Even though it was the dead of winter, this was a delicacy I could savour year round.

Coco and I watched, leering through the bars in disbelief that we were not being included. Minutes later they returned to eat

a lab report

their cones and nougat wafers in the car as it was too cold to hang about outside. At one point mean Megan held hers up high when she was speaking excitedly about something and I took the liberty of squeezing my tongue through the bars and giving it a full on greedy lick. I got that instant brain freeze from the cold and screwed my eyes up to contend with the pain. It was gone in a flash but was instantly replaced by another pain...

"Rosie's licked my ice cream," balled Megan.

Not my fault. Even Amy and Rob must have been able to configure this as Megan had to have almost gifted it to me to allow me to secure that lick through my prison bars. To put her lungs to bed, poor Rob was sent, by Amy, to buy her another. That meant, in my calculations, she got one ice cream and a bit (the bit before I managed to get my lick). Conniving little minx.

The boot opened and there stood Amy, brandishing the remnants of Megan's first ice cream. Coco, being the eldest, got the first few licks and then I got the rest, cone and all. Yum, yum, my belly was numb. I sank down and curled up between Coco and the ruckie, after creating the ruckus. I needed to be Cosy Rosie Posie for the journey home.

Once home, there was only sufficient enough time for a quick lunch of soup and bacon rolls before Mike, Emma and the minis headed off to Aberdeenshire for the rest of their holidays and to see New Year in with their other rellies. Just before they all headed off Amy was keen to let the kids see my latest trick, which involved some yoghurt being dangled off a spoon, from about a metre above my head. I had to watch it carefully and deduce when it was going to slide off the spoon, before sticking out my tongue like a lizard, to catch it before it splattered on the floor. Not the worst case scenario as I could lick it up from there too.

So there I was, alongside Coco and Bubby, both well-rehearsed artists at this game, who went first to show how it was done. For me you see, it was a bit of a hit or miss. Sometimes it landed like a ball on my nose, other times on my head, which Coco and Bubby then licked off as my tongue, although long, was unable to curl round and lick it off myself. I focused on the spoon, like a performing buffoon and waited on the timely dropping of my creamy, vanilla-tasting Greek yoghurt (only the best for us). One, two, three, off it fell. Tongue out - I caught most of it, with less than half going on my nose - which in itself was a huge achievement. The kids cheered,

"Again, again!"

I got another go. Mouth agape, I moved under the spoon like a fireman waiting to catch a child jumping on to a safety rug from a high building. A little movement here and there for fine tuning until it dropped off, landing straight in to my mouth with me swallowing it over. I licked my lips gleefully.

"Again, more, more," chanted the kids.

"I think Rosie's had enough for the time being. It wouldn't do for her to be over fed and get fat. Labradors are, by nature, greedy dogs and I wouldn't want to encourage her too much."

Bit late for that I thought or you wouldn't have taught me 'the yoghurt trick' you think so amusing you posted it on YouTube! (Since my human cousins have returned to Australia,

a lab report

when we speak across the miles on Skype or FaceTime, they always request for me to perform my yoghurt trick. I am always extremely happy to oblige - for the youngsters sake of course rather than the opportunity to get more food legitimately).

Mike and Emma had now packed up all the baggage and gifts and taken them out to the car so it was time to say aurevoir mes amis. With hugs and kisses all round, even to us dogs, they all headed out to the car, along with my human granny, whom they were dropping off en route. I wandered out to the car with Amy, who was walking hand in hand with Megan, who had spent the last ten minutes glued to Brambles' side, cuddling, kissing and telling her how much she loved her.

As I danced a merry dance alongside Amy and Megan my ears tuned in to a conversation I didn't really understand.

"You will phone and let me know as soon as Brambles dies?" quizzed Megan.

Amy took a minute or two to answer, and it seemed to me that she was choking back some tears.

"Of course I will, honey. Let's just hope that's not too soon".

"Me too," smiled Megan, at the same time as wrapping her arms around Amy's legs and cuddling them tightly.

They were all in the car now, Coco was at Rob's side and he had picked me up, for safety I am sure, and was holding me tightly in his arms. No fear of me running away with that mad bunch, even though it had been fun. I did like kids in my own kind of way - particularly as they fed you on the fly. The only pity was you couldn't remove their batteries like Amy and Rob could with some of my toys.

"Bye, love you," was being shouted from all angles.

Rob waved my paw for me. The car had now reversed out the drive and they were facing the main road. Arms were waving frantically out of windows.

"Safe journey. Loved having you!" shouted Amy, who was now cuddled in to Rob, tears running down her cheeks. She must be sad to see her sister go I thought. I would know that feeling myself in a few months' time. The only difference being, she would see hers again.

I ran back inside and nestled in to Bubby at the fireside. Sweet dreams in the peace and tranquillity of the kid free zone.

18

New Year

A few months had now passed since Daniel, Steven and Megan had returned home to Australia but every time I spotted a child playing on any of my walks, I would run up to them thinking it was one of them. I'd be about to give them a big smackeroo on their face, or steal their hat, when I'd hear Amy, Rob or some parent screaming at me. What was their problem? I was just being friendly.

The children had turned my life upside down, and inside out, and had had a massive effect on us all, to the extent that they had even cheered Brambles up, so much so that her spirit remained high for about a month afterwards on the love, care and attention that

Megan had drowned her in. Rob and Amy chatted to her, gave her cuddles and kisses but were a tad too large to squeeze in to Bubby's bed like Megan had. She had spent literally every waking moment being Brambles' best buddy and it appeared to be a truly symbiotic relationship. My relationships were more parasitic and mainly revolved around food.

A few days ago Rob had watched me practising my hunter-gatherer skills when I managed to use my nose to sniff out a spider on the decking, trap it with my paw and then gobble it up. One less in the world for the arachniphobics to worry about. Admittedly, it was not the most nutritious, filling or tasty meal I have ever laid my lips around but I had read that it was better to have a little often than one heavy meal, which would limit my mobility for chasing and end up giving me a twisted stomach. Given I am domesticated, although I know sometimes this may seem debatable, my animalistic survival skills still need to be practised and honed to supplement my diet.

With just Amy and Rob left to amuse me, life returned to its usual humdrum, although I did my best to add some spice to it through my various misdemeanours. When the kids had been here it had been easy to blame them for wrongdoings - not that anyone ever believed it was anyone else but me when Flakey and Snowy had been decimated - but now I was on my own again there was definitely no one to pass the buck to.

February brought a distinct decline in Bubby's overall health and I was stopped from doing my usual blasting out of bed and tearing down the stairs to greet her. I was taught about respecting the elderly and infirm. That meant that I was still allowed to race

a lab report

down to see Coco, give her a few paw bops on the head, and then return to Bubby's bedside, now at the foot of the hall stairs, to stare quietly at her in her bed, looking for any trace of a rise and fall in her rib cage to signal she was still alive. As she was so deaf now she rarely heard any movement round about her and the only way to wake her up was to use one of her other senses, smell, which I believe no dog loses even as it ages. Just as well, as that would ruin our ability to sniff out food to scrounge.

Rob would stand motionless alongside her bed, observing her, then drop down to his knees and wave his hand up and down in front of her nostrils, hoping to stir her gently so as not to frighten or alarm her. To the contrary, I was Rob's rude awakening and was a true Pavlovian dog, conditioned to respond to his six am alarm call by pouncing on him if he took more than a few nano-seconds to get up to feed me. At least he was assured of never sleeping in; on the odd occasion he'd forgotten to set his clock I was still true to form waking bang on schedule. How's that for proving the theory of conditioning?

Once Bubby's nostrils started puffing in and out and sniffing Rob's hand, he'd stroke her whole body, from head down to tail, until she was more compos mentis and her eyes were as wide open as any old dog's ever were. Why do dogs not get glasses like humans to help them see better in their older years? Or contact lenses? It seems to me that medical advancements and care of ageing dogs are lagging behind human 'palliative' care. We just get the 'pal' part instead. Well, I get Beta Puppy. Better than that tinned stuff!

Rob would then assist her to her feet by supporting her under her hips and stabilising her. The first stop would be an amble out to the garden to do the necessary acts. Sometimes she'd even trip over a blade of grass her legs were so weak. Unable to raise herself up again, Rob was there, like her knight in shining armour, to help her back on to her shaky pins. It was terribly sad to see her slowing down so much and I wondered why dogs weren't given zimmers or mobility scooters to help them get around more easily. She could then have come walks with us and I could catch a lift from her when I got puggled after chasing bunnies, squirrels or even Coco. On second thoughts, Brambles could race the scooter after Coco, with me sitting alongside her at the helm, teaming up together. This would give Brambles that much needed spirit of adventure important in keeping old dogs young at heart; a sense of mischief that only a menace like me could foster in her. I knew I would never need to worry about getting old as I just knew that would never happen to me; I would be like a fine wine, remaining ageless and getting more refined and tastier with every passing year.

Through wonderful care and attention by Amy and Rob, Brambles was still very much alive on March 9th, the date the most amazing creature on earth was born. Yes, me! It was my first birthday. Bubby and Coco had sent me a card, with some dire joke on the front of it, which wasn't remotely funny and was obviously selected on their behalf by Rob, who had a sick sense of humour. They had both signed it with muddy paw-prints and there was a ten pound note tucked inside it, which I used to buy fish with, for our dinner - generous to a fault - that's me! Coco and I ate all of ours and Bubby made as good an attempt as she could, not wanting

a lab report

to insult my generosity being my special birthday tea. Even though she was still being hand fed she only consumed pickings, which were not even enough to sustain a tea cup Chihuahua, never mind a big dog like her. If I'd had a set of drum sticks, I would have been able to play 'Happy Birthday To Me' on her xylophone ribs. On one hand I felt sorry she didn't have a bigger appetite but on the other hand I didn't wish to protest too profusely as our dishes were always replenished with her left overs.

My sisters had also gifted me a new toy for my birthday. It was a red dinosaur which I named Dino for short. Thinking outside of the box or what? Apparently he was a Velociraptor, which when translated from its Latin, (I am very good at Latin), means 'fast thief'. I would need to keep a close eye on Dino now that there were two of us in the same household!

Dino had a frilly neck and humungous white gnashing teeth, which made my own look like needles in a haystack. He could have been perceived as scary but I knew he wasn't real so he didn't phase me at all. When I was a really wee puppy Coco had tried to frighten me by telling me that my toys came alive at night and if I hadn't treated them nicely, they would eat me alive. For that reason I used to sleep with one eye open and one closed, interchanging them throughout the night, just to make sure I was still there in the morning. It was Vinny Van Patch who told me, when we chatted in my bed one night, that Coco was just winding me up and that was rubbish. Coco then asked me how Vinny, who was only a toy, could tell me that if he wasn't alive? I tried not to think about that too much.

All in all, I had a wonderful first birthday as my collie 'friends' came in the afternoon to join us for a walk at the beach. I use the words 'friends' loosely as they were more associates, in the sense that they were Amy's friend's dogs, and like most parents who got together with their friends, their kids were just expected to play together and get on. Not my particular choice of pals but I was more than happy to welcome them on this memorable day if it resulted in them bearing gifts, and not their teeth as 'Smiler', the middle aged one of the trio, often did. When my gift was presented to me I was half expecting it to be another sheep, to add to the one previously given to me by them at Christmas. Would two give me a flock? I could not get overly excited at the prospect of opening their gift, given they never play with toys, so took my time peeling back the gift wrap knowing their choice was bound to be a duff one. I took a deep breath in when I revealed a Collie dog toy, which looked exactly like them. Black and white with a stupid grin on its face, just like smiler. Wonderful! I would now be able to show them what I could do to one of them if they messed with me in the future as I tore in to Cyril (as you know all my toys have a name) and flung him around a bit by the scruff. Vicious, that's me!

My birthday celebrations finished with us all, well not Amy and Rob, getting a bit of my designer birthday cake, which Amy had bought from some special retailers who made Doggy Birthday Cakes from biscuit bones. How healthy, if not a bit boring. Now a big, gooey chocolate cake would have been much more in keeping with my special day - even if it had to be doggie chocolate.

Amy lit the one candle on my cake and got me to try and

a lab report

blow it out as she and Rob sung Happy Birthday to me. You will be amazed to learn that I couldn't manage this myself, so it was done for me. Why have a Rob and blow it out yourself? After making a wish, Amy divided the cake up in to chunks for me and my chums. It was lip-smacking good and I noticed that there was enough to last a few suppers, to eke out my birthday celebrations for a while longer..........

As the days and weeks passed I would often overhear Rob and Amy discussing whether it 'was time' for Bubby. I didn't really perceive the significance of what they were referring to but could sense, as we dogs can from tuning in to human's emotional responses, that it wasn't something Amy wanted as she would continually get upset every time the topic arose. I heard her utter that she would struggle to euthanase her when mentally she was still as bright as a button yet she was fading away right in front of her eyes. The conversation would terminate at this point as Amy was unable to converse further through her torrent of tears. For Amy, Brambles had been her loving, faithful, yet bone-idle companion for fourteen years. She didn't want to have to contemplate life without her, nor have to make that phone call to Megan.

Days passed and events over took any decisions they had to make, as it seemed Bubby had decided to take matters in to her own hands.

It was April 3rd, almost a month after my birthday, and I was playing happily out in the garden with Amy and Coco, running after a ball and taunting Coco with it in my mouth, to goad her for a chase. From nowhere came a shrill call from inside the house.

"Amy... Amy, come quickly."

Amy took to her heels, and without a second to lose me and Coco joined her and sprinted inside to find Rob kneeling at Brambles' side. He was stroking her coat and she was looking up at him in a confused manner. Her eyes seemed empty and lost.

Rob went on to explain, "She just collapsed. Her legs went from right under her."

Amy was also down at Bubby's side now, using her hand to stroke her head and then cupping her face in her hands.

"I love you honey bun," she said. "But it hurts me so much to see you going through all of this. I need to let you go somewhere happier. Somewhere where you can play in the grass, run free again. Jay and Holly will be there to greet you and look after you."

I shut my eyes and thought about what she was saying. I knew Jay and Holly had been previous dogs of Amy's and maybe she had to give them away at some point and Bubby was going to be given away to the same place. At least she'd have pals I thought. Why couldn't me and Coco go too?

Rob looked at Amy and without hesitation, even though there were tears welling in his eyes too, he said,

"I will phone the vet in the morning and ask them to come to the house. We both know it's time and the kindest thing to do. Let's just enjoy her for tonight and make it as special and comfortable as we can for her."

With that, he got up and left Amy caressing and cuddling her. Coco and I returned to the garden to continue playing ball, with no concept of the enormity of today's events and what was about to unfold tomorrow.

a lab report

19

April 4th

Even though I had witnessed Amy and Rob upset I was a far too happy go lucky dog to ever feel sad. That was, until today. On the face of it, it seemed like every other day. We got up, had breakfast, did our business and returned to speak to Bubby in her bed in the hall. Rob went off to make a phone call and returned to tell Amy that Lucy would be here about half past midday. Amy had been tearful off and on all the previous evening and when he gave her this message, she broke down again, and he hugged her close, trying to reassure her that they were making the right decision. It was kinder for Brambles he told her. Hearing only half the conversations that were going on, I was more than a little confused about what was happening. I only knew one person called Lucy, who was my vet, and wondered why she would possibly be coming to my house.

Coco and I had our collars clipped around our necks and were taken for a brisk walk round the local estate. When we returned, Bubby was cosied up in front of the fire on my sheepskin vet bed. It was really mine to lie on but, on this occasion, I decided to leave her on it and just curl up beside her. There was room enough for two and she always gave out a lot of warmth so was a good, snuggly bed buddy.

It was now eleven am and Amy and Rob seemed to be fussing around doing a lot of nothing. Bubby had decided to get up herself, seeming more sprightly than usual, and had wandered out to the garden, via the dog flap, and was standing inhaling deep breathfuls of air in to her lungs. This was quite bizarre and uncharacteristic of late as she barely moved from her bed unaided. Following a quick widdle, she returned through the flap and back to her mat, or should I say my mat, in the living-room. It was cool out today and the best place to be was in front of the roaring fire. As Bubby was so thin these days she was always assured of the prime spot, as even if I was on it, I was turfed off by Rob or Amy in favour of her or at least made to share. A bit like the unwritten rule or etiquette expected in relation to giving up your seat to the elderly on the bus. I always would struggle with this seeing as I had paid my fare and they had got it free gratis. Never mind, not one to lose too much sleep over.

As Bubby baked in front of the fire Amy curled up beside

a lab report

her, cuddling her and repeatedly telling her how much she loved her. I think Bubby, and the rest of us, got the message loud and clear. Suddenly, Amy sat up and announced cheerily to Bubby,

"I am going to send you out on your favourite snack. It won't matter at this stage."

With that she disappeared through to the sweetie cupboard in the kitchen, where the jelly babies and wine gums were kept, and appeared back in a few minutes with a small packet of Cadbury's milk chocolate buttons (it could only be Cadbury's - everyone's favourite). As she opened it up, Bubby pushed herself to her feet and sat bolt upright, having smelt the delicacy she was about to be receive.

"Enjoy," Amy said smiling as she extracted chocolate button after chocolate button, and fed them to Bubby, who ate every single one, including mopping up the crumbs she had dropped. She was certainly relishing, what was to be, her last supper.

Apparently chocolate is toxic to dogs and Amy had only found this out after reading a book on things dogs can and can't eat. The list was endless; onions (I think dogs choose not to eat them anyway because they are so bitter and make your breath stink to high heaven); grapes, prunes (make you go to the toilet - not good); and so the list went on. Anyway, after reading it, chocolate was removed from our diet entirely and that also applied to my human granny, who was no longer allowed to bring us our white milky buttons, unless they were the doggy chocolate ones, which were minging in comparison to the real McCoy. Amy's old dog, Squally (Holly by birth), used to take her packet of milky buttons, from her human granny, out to the garden and bury them, digging them up some days later to consume as a special treat. No other dog ever knew where they were as the days in-between eating them she continuously moved their location. How smart was that?!

Another story, proving how motivated dogs are to eat chocolate, was when Rob and Amy had first started dating and they had gone out and left their two dogs together. Whilst they were out they got up to high jinx, sniffing out and consuming a Terry's dark chocolate orange and a Cadbury's selection box between them, only leaving some foil wrapping as evidence of their exploits. Both Rob and Amy had been bemused by this at the time and it was only years later that they realised the potential harm it could have caused the dogs. However neither was up nor down and both lived to the ripe old age of fourteen, a good age for greedy black Labradors. Now, if they had been chocolate Labradors, would they have lived even longer?

After Brambles had eaten all her chocolate Rob fed her some gravy bones and then she got some cheddar cheese. I thought chocolate and cheese together could cause migraines? Even if they did, I would be willing to risk it as it sounded like a heavenly combination.

Bubby had enjoyed her very own buffet. She had gobbled the whole lot over and seemed to be storing it like a squirrel who was about to go in to hibernation for months. Coco and I did not get even one morsel and the result of living in hope had been litres of drool, like the flowing waterfall at Niagara Falls, which had created a pool on the floor and would have easily floated Maid of the Mist.

a lab report

Having eventually had her fill, Brambles curled back down on the mat, shut her eyes and went off to sleep.

'Ding, dong'

The bell had sounded and Coco started to bark and ran through to the hall, waiting inside the front door waiting for it to be answered. I hovered in the living room doorway to see who it was.

"That'll be Lucy," Rob shouted through to Amy,

"She's early. It 's only ten past twelve and she said she wasn't coming until half past. I am not ready for this yet......I thought I still had twenty minutes," Amy retorted in a muffled voice.

The door had now been opened and Rob was ushering Lucy and the strange vet nurse in to the hallway. When I say 'strange' she wasn't funny looking or anything, I just hadn't seen her before. I was quite glad Lucy hadn't brought Rosie with her as I had gone off her a bit since my last visit to the vet when they had sewn up my belly. It's funny how you lose trust in someone when they double-cross you, even if you do share a name. It is a fallacy that all people called the same name as you are as nice as you!

Coco continued to bark at the vet nurse but I was likely to be needing some medicare of my own soon as I was all over Lucy like a rash. Coco didn't seem to be as taken with their visit as me, although I was still trying to work out why they were here.

"She's in the living-room with Amy," Rob pointed the way forward.

Happy to assist, I darted in front of them to show them the way, wagging my tail as I went, quite pleased with having one of my own friends to the house for once. Brambles was sitting up on the mat now, looking quite bright and as Lucy entered the room, the tip of her tail gave a small wag. Amy was sitting next to her with one arm draped across her back and her free hand was stroking the top of Bubby's head over and over, as if to keep her calm.

"Aww............." Lucy said in a long drawn out, sad tone, at the same time as placing her case on one of the chairs and proceeding to open it. As she did so I poked my nose inside it, sniffed some of the instruments and just as I made an attempt to prise out a small bag of cotton wool pads, Rob grabbed a hold of me and pulled me out to the hall, shutting the door firmly behind me. I now stood alongside Coco, peering in through the glass to see what I was missing out on.

I spotted a stethoscope around Lucy's neck, which she was holding to Brambles' chest. I knew she was using this to listen to her heartbeat as Lucy had sounded me when she had done my first ever health check when I was a young pup. I had a heart then.

After Lucy had finished doing this Rob changed places with Amy, who proceeded to get up from the floor and wander aimlessly back and fore across the room, looking like she was trying to ignore what was going on right under her nose, except for stealing the odd quick glance in their direction. She never once looked to see what me and Coco were up to outside the door.

In exchange for the stethoscope, the nameless vet nurse passed Lucy an electric razor - I was familiar with these - and Lucy was now in the process of shaving a bit of hair off Brambles' leg and creating a bald patch on it. After passing the razor back to the vet nurse, she handed her a rubber band, which she then tied round

a lab report

the top of Bubby's leg and then she used a wet tissue to rub some ointment on the shaven patch. I had seen old men rub their hankies on the bald patches on their heads too in what I believed to be an attempt to generate hair. Given she had just shaved Brambles' hair I didn't think she would be rubbing a hair growth stimulating hormone on to her leg so guessed it must have been for something else - quite what, I wasn't sure.

Rob was now looking up at Amy, and I heard him say to her,

"Amy, you should be holding her. She's your dog and she trusts you most. You should be with her at this point. Come on....."
He tapped the floor beside him, got up and swapped places with a very unwilling Amy.

Once she was seated and holding Bubby close, I watched quietly as Amy took a moment or two to kiss her head and then I heard her tell her,

"I love you so much, honey bun. I will miss you so much. Sweet dreams."

Lucy had now inserted a long, sharp needle in to Bubby's baldy bit and was using her thumb to press the end of the jag towards her leg, squeezing liquid in to it. Brambles was leaning against Amy, who had one arm around her shoulder and the other hand continued to stroke her head and ears. I pressed my face harder against the glass door and started to whimper a bit. I could see tears cascading from Amy's eyes and falling on Bubby's coat. Her body was shaking and I noticed Brambles' body had started to slump down on to the floor; whatever Lucy was pumping in to her was obviously making her feel tired. Her nostrils were flailing and her chest rising and falling deeply, as if trying to get more air in. Amy, who had been supporting her head, lowered it gently to the ground and she helped Bubby, with her hands, to curl up in to a cosy, sleeping position on the rug. She then looked up at Rob. For a moment in time, everything seemed to hang in space and there was a haunting silence.

Amy had her hands clasped up in front of her mouth now, and I noticed her eyes glistening, full of liquid, which when she blinked, dripped down her cheeks like rain running down a window pane. They continued to fall like heavy rain on a dreich day - which it was. I use this great Scottish word as no other word exists to replace the sentiments it conveys.

I saw Lucy retrieve her stethoscope from her bag and place it to Brambles' chest. She kept it there for what seemed like a lifetime.

"That's her away," Lucy whispered softly, looking up at Amy and Rob.

She rose slowly, placing both the stethoscope and injection back in her case, closed the lid and said to them,

"I'll give you both a minute or two with her."

She then opened the door, and went outside, with her stranger, leaving me and Coco able to go back in to the living-room to suss out what was really going on.

I tore in, as ever, but Coco hung back at the door, opting to stay outside and away from the main action. Whereas me, I always preferred to be in the thick of things - as you know!

Amy and Rob were huddled around Bubby who seemed to

a lab report

be sleeping soundly and oblivious to all that was going on beside her. Amy was still crying and I tried my best to lick her tears dry but they were still falling faster than I could cope with. Plus, there was only so much salt I could cope with before it made my tongue so dry my own slavers started to dry up. Not good. I watched as Amy took a hankie out her pocket, wiped her eyes and then blew her nose fiercely, and returned it back to her pocket. I then stuck my nose in, pinched it and ran off with it, with her calling after me,

"Not today, Rosie please."

But by that time, it was swallowed over and in my tum, tum. Rob squeezed her, telling her not to be too hard on me as I was too young to understand what was going on. He managed to get a small teary smile from her as she said,

"I know. Everything's just one big game to Rosie Posie. She loved Brambles too in her own way."

He squeezed her close again, as if in agreement. They were right in some ways. Life was one big party to me but I was clever enough to know something wasn't right and with a little more guidance, I would work it out, or Coco would tell me, as older sisters should.

"Coco come," beckoned Amy.

Coco crept in to the living-room and sidled up to beside Amy and Rob. She looked distinctly uncomfortable though.

"Coco, that's your sister gone to her new home in the sky. Come and say goodbye."

Coco lingered for about a second, and following a quick look at Bubby, about turned and left the room. Weird. I was then summoned to see her. Once at her side, I put my nose down towards her, sniffed her coat and licked her ear. She felt warm and cosy and I wondered when she would decide to wake up. As if reading my thoughts Rob pulled me towards him, hugged me tightly, and explained,

"She's not going to up wake up Rosie Posie however much you lick her. No kiss of life is going to bring her back - not even yours."

Just at that point, Lucy arrived back without the vet nurse, after putting her bag in her car.

"Are you both okay? Have you had long enough with her or do you want some more time?"

"We're fine," commented Rob. "I'll carry her out to the car."

He bent down, picked Brambles up and swathed her in a large, multi-coloured towel he used to dry her with when she returned from her muddy, wet walks. I still kept my eyes firmly fixed on her, looking at her the whole time he wrapped her up, which he did so like he was wrapping up a special gift, which she has been for the last fourteen years. I willed her to wake up and bark 'boo' like she had just been pretending to sleep. But she wasn't. She was dead to the world.

Amy pulled back the towel a little to reveal her face, gave her one last kiss on the head, and placed the cover back gently. She then turned away, wiping her face dry with a fresh hankie, which was now sodden, and kept it squeezed in her hand.

I chummed Rob out to Lucy's car, where he placed Brambles carefully and lovingly in to her boot, shutting the lid when he

a lab report

had finished doing so. This felt so similar to when we had waved goodbye to Megan and the others, but even worse. My sister was going away forever and there was this overwhelming sadness gripping my chest. This was the first time in my existence I had felt anything other than happiness. I didn't like feeling like this and hoped it would go away soon.

After thanking Lucy, and without waiting to see them off, Rob hurried back in to the house, with me running behind him to keep up. Once inside, and with the door closed to the world, he crumbled on to the first step of the stair case, put his head in his hands and sobbed his heart out. I sat quietly beside him, not uttering a sound. Amy was still in the living-room sitting on the same spot where Brambles had been only minutes ago, vital with life still oozing through her veins; in ten minutes that had changed - all of our lives had changed from this moment onwards.

I had never seen either of them so openly distressed before and I didn't know what to do to make them feel any better. Probably because I couldn't deal with the enormity of what had just happened either as it felt like the stuffing had been picked out of me. I yearned to turn the clock back to make all this sadness go away, but I knew, that as wonderful as I was, even I could not do that. I got up from Rob's side and started to scour the house for Coco. I didn't have to look very far before I located her. She was curled up in Bubby's bed and instinctively I knew why. It was her way of feeling close to the thing she loved and had just lost. Coco kept her own counsel; she was deep and had never been one to bare her soul, her teeth yes, but this was her way of telling us that she was in mourning too. Who said dogs don't have feelings?

The intensity of a dog's loyalty to their soul mate has always been questioned and it is easy for those people without a true understanding of dogs to argue that it was just coincidence that Coco had chosen to lie in Brambles' bed or that she was an opportunist. I may have said that too until today when I experienced the emotions associated with bereavement myself. However, knowing what I know now, I profess that dogs have emotions similar to humans and that comes straight from the mouth of the biggest chancer, me! This theory is also borne out in a story I overheard Amy recount to Rob when she had also found Coco seeking solace in Brambles' bed. She told him that one of her previous dogs had gone on a hunger strike for a week after her companion had been put to sleep at the vets and not returned home. She had spent days looking for her before deciding she was never coming back. It was from that day forward that Amy had decided that the other dogs must always know that their life long companion has died to be able to move on with their life too.

Now I understood why the vet had come to our house and it became crystal clear to me why Coco had been less than pleased to see her. She had been through this before. If there was ever to be a next time, and she came for Coco, there was no way she was getting in. She should count herself officially barred from this house by me from this day forward.

The rest of the day was very subdued and even on our walk Coco wasn't up for chasing or playing. Suddenly I only had one big sister to boss around. My meals would also go back to being plain

a lab report

and ordinary, with no titbits, now the gourmet eater was no longer in the equation. On that note, I tottered through to Bubby's bed in the study; surely she must have left a biscuit in it for me.

20

Allergies

It was official. I am different, which is the kind word for a mutant.

My allergies started a few weeks after Brambles died. It was mid April and I had started to lose clumps of hair from various parts of my body. I was going bald on my tummy, under my arm pits and the tips of my ears. I would scratch myself stupid, for no apparent reason, and must have looked as though I was going a bit deranged. Rob and Amy immediately jumped to the wrong conclusion that it was a stress disorder brought about by grief and mourning Bubby. Rather than taking me to the vet they thought the obvious answer was just to lavish more attention on me, which

a lab report

in turn would cheer me up and 'sort' me out. If only life were so simple.

Me being me, I loved the extra attention - I mean, who doesn't like being the centre of the universe? I got immense pleasure from being petted and patted; it was like having my own personal fan club at my beck and call. To milk it I would sit on the floor, reach up and use my paw to grab their hands down to tickle my alopecia belly. It was seventh heaven. As soon as they stopped, my paw would immediately go up again to enable me to receive more gratification. After about an hour they'd eventually send me packing.

Two weeks later, nothing had changed and it would be fair to say my situation was deteriorating - I was still shedding my coat. It was at this point Amy took me along to my less-than-favourite friend, the vet. She diagnosed it as a mite problem. It might be this, or it might be that! No, really, she believed that some wee bug had infested my system and was causing an allergic reaction of some sort so she suggested a week of antibiotics and to bring me back after they finished to see how things were settling down.

A week later there was no obvious change. My hair was not growing back in, nor had I stopped scratching. Lucy took a swab of saliva, easy to get this from me at any stage - just show me a biscuit - and she also shaved a bit of my coat - more hair loss, and took a skin swab. These were sent off to the lab. Aren't we dogs so clever; even a Lab analysed my medical problems. Is there is no end to our versatility.

We returned a few days later for the results. It was positive for allergies but a more detailed analysis would have to be carried out to be able to identify what these were caused by. Probably that dusty hall I had done my obedience in all that time ago! Bad things can have a lasting effect.

At this point I was referred on to an Allergy Specialist called Eric Watson. The initial consultation fee was £500. Now that meant nothing to me as I didn't deal in hard cash, just treats. It must have been a lot though as I heard Amy take a sharp intake of breath. I also spotted Rob raising his eyebrows at her. Just as well I was insured! Such precious things always are.

Eric was so highly thought of and sought after by all the allergen dogs that I was told it could take until August to get my first appointment with him - a whole four months - just as well my hair loss had plateaued or I would have been completely bald like some of these shaven dogs at Crufts. Cold or what? My initial appointment would last for up to two hours to afford him copious amounts of time to examine me and carry out routine skin tests. Why did the medical profession refer to them as routine? There was certainly nothing routine about them for me.

Luckily for me, I got a cancellation at the start of May. I arrived five minutes early for my appointment with Eric and waited in a rather dull and boring waiting room compared to my own. There were no toys or other animals to play with (I worked out later on that this was probably so I didn't catch other dogs' bugs) and the nurses never even came and spoke to me - maybe in case they thought I was contagious? The vibes were less than friendly, more fiendly in fact - not good anyway. I had made up my mind I

a lab report

didn't like this place.

A man appeared in a white coat and called my name, "Rosie Maxwell."

Just call me Rosie I wanted to say, let's drop this officialdom. He introduced himself to Amy and Rob as Eric Watson, and then we proceeded to follow in his big foot steps, through to the consulting room. The door was closed behind us and I took a moment or two to look around; no posters or treats visible. So much for trying to keep me de-stressed and make it a welcoming environment.

Eric popped me up on the table, placed his hands on me and rolled them around my body as he fired twenty million questions at Rob and Amy. When did the allergy start? Were there specific times it flared up? Had my food changed recently? Where was I walked? Where did I sleep? I looked straight at him at that point. I drew the line at that highly intrusive question! The questions rolled on and on until Eric had built up the bigger picture of my lifestyle. He then explained that he was going to give me a reversible anaesthetic, shave a section of my side and carry out a skin test against the sixteen most common allergens. He relayed them all to us which ranged from soap (I never washed so wondered why this was included), grass, mud, house-mites, dust mites and bed bugs. Very heavily weighted in one direction I felt! He explained that the allergen dots which turned bright orange showed a positive reaction, and the ones remaining yellow were negative.

Once I had been anaesthetised, shaved, dotted in everything imaginable, I had a stressful hour's wait hanging about to see which ones flared up. It had better not be the food ones or life wouldn't be worth contemplating.

The results returned a roaring bright orange/positive for house and dust mites. When Eric told Amy this she reacted quite angrily, retorting that she kept a very clean house, hoovering and cleaning every day. Eric went on to explain that even the cleanest of houses have house-mites and dust-mites and this was not a personal slight on her.

Eric posed a question,

"What did these results mean in terms of keeping me hale and hearty?"

This was the most important thing after all. He stressed that to the best of their ability, they were to stop me sleeping on carpets, in furry dogs' beds and certainly not, he impressed strongly, in bedrooms or on human beds, as they hold the most housemites of any place in the house! Woo, hoo! I was ecstatic. I was now going to be turfed out of my sleeping quarters. I thought back to my earlier times of sharing Amy and Rob's room and expressing my own concerns when Amy had flung her duvet back that time and I had got covered in her fleas. That must have been the start of my allergies. Would she be treated as well then I wondered? A bit like nits, all the household have to be treated if they are to be eradicated or it just becomes cyclical as it moves from one to another.

He then elaborated, saying I could sleep on leather, wood, and at a push, these special vet beds. If it was to be a vet bed, it must be washed weekly at ninety degrees to kill any bugs. Amy and Rob asked him, if any, what my treatment would be beyond the control

a lab report

measures in the house. What he then told them was almost run away unbelievable! I was to have two anti-histamine tablets a day - one with breakfast and one with my dinner; fine I thought, a form of food so easy enough to swallow them over. I had to have my feet sprayed every Monday, Tuesday and Wednesday night. I was miffed that I hadn't been diagnosed earlier as that might have meant I would have been unable to attend those deadly boring, almost death-inducing obedience classes, as it would have coincided with one of the nights my feet were being sprayed. The dust in that hall must have been a mitigating factor in terms of inducing allergies in any healthy dog too. I am sure there were more dust mites in that hall than you could shake a brush or mop at. Although the new spraying regime would coincide with my pending agility training evening, which was to start in June, given the edibles at the field Coco had enlightened me about, I was happy to adopt a flexible approach and have them sprayed post session.

I would also require an injection once a month, which he was going to show Amy how to give me. This injection was a dose of my allergy to try and help me build up some resistance to it. Why treat me with all the other drugs I thought if you are just going to blow all that to pieces by injecting me with housemites to which I am allergic? Crazy dude!

Finally, wait for it; I was to have the pleasure of a shower and shampoo in the bath every Saturday night. The shampoo would have to be massaged in for ten minutes and then rinsed off then I was to be left to dry naturally. The curtains and cover along the sofa would aid me with this as I usually ran along these to dry myself off anyway when Amy or Rob hadn't done a very good job with the towel after we came back from walks. What are a few mud marks between friends? Preferable to skid marks I am sure.

There were a whole more set of rules and regulations to be followed and I got bored listening but noticed Amy and Rob hanging on every word he uttered. I was to be shut out the house when it was hoovered and ideally not allowed back in for two hours afterwards so if I could be walked at this point that would be helpful. Oh, and, if they could buy a Dyson Animal Hoover, with a hepa filter, that would also help to control my allergies. I am sure that they probably wanted to use the hoover, so aptly named 'animal', to sook me up right at this moment given the time and expense of my treatment! Just as well I was insured or I may have been sent out with my begging bowl. Although on saying that, I would have had to be very selective about what I could take on now given my allergies as I am sure they could be brought on very easily. Work in itself would probably have a profoundly detrimental effect.

I had other ideas to help keep my allergies in check. The straw in my kennel should be changed for padded leather flooring, so I was comfortable. I would have to get my own leather settee or they would have to renege in their strict policy of no dogs on seats so I could join them on their one. One up again Coco Loco! The whole house was going to be run for me from now on, just as it should be. I was going to have the cleanest house on earth with no mites of any kind.

Finally, Eric said he would like to see me back after six months, in approximately November, to check how I was getting on with my treatment.

21

Gullane (Part One)

It was the middle of May and I was now just over fourteen months old; big enough and ugly enough - to coin a phrase - as I was not ugly, to venture off the lead now that I was a Kennel Club affiliated silver obedience award pooch. A deaf ear and a blind eye at times, detracted from this fact, but it still remained, I was now so highly trained I could be recruited by the SAS, MI6 or even DOGS. (Have you managed to work this acronym out yet. If you have, well done as I made it up!)

Once we arrived at Gullane and Rob opened the boot, Coco barged her way out first and ran straight over to the bunny bushes with me in hot pursuit. Her tail wagged constantly and now that she was getting a white beard and moustache she bore more resemblance to a skunk than a Lab. She also smelt like one at times when her flatulence was at its peak after evening meal times which offered a day's pent up gases, which were also made up of all the rubbish she had consumed on her walks. Poo... eeeeee!

Rather than waste too much time on bunny hunting in the bush (as you know I have Aussie rellies), I headed straight to the picnic tables to scavenge for leftovers. I was always lucky. One day I found a whole packet of cheesy wotsits which made my breath smell for days. I liked cheese in any shape and form; so much so that all my neighbours had stopped putting it out for the birds now that they were aware that the rare Rosie blackbird consumed it when she flew by.

Sometimes there would be BBQs left behind too and I would do my best, in the few seconds I had before Amy or Rob grabbed my collar, to lick the tops of these and savour the flavour of the charcoaled offerings. Why they called them 'disposable' I'd never know as I certainly couldn't manage to swallow them over. It seemed that some people took the disposable part literally and being synonymous with vanishing - thinking that someone else would make them disappear if they left them behind. I suppose dogs such as my good self helped in this chain of events, as to prevent me spending all day at these discarded grills, Amy and Rob would lift them up and dispose of them in the nearest bins. Job done!

Some days we would walk along the cliff tops to the bay at the west end of the main beach. Other days we would speed down the steep brae taking us to the main beach and run along eastwards

a lab report

towards North Berwick. This was the best way when summer came as I stood the utmost chance of stealing children's crocs or wellies if they had been left unattended when they paddled in the sea. I loved lolloping in to the water and joining them.

One day there were three boys in their shorts, wading in to the ocean up to their waists trying not to get too wet too quickly to allow their bodies to adjust to the freezing temperature. 'Come on boys,' I thought - Men or mice? So I flicked my paws a few times, like a bull about to chase the matador, and ran full pelt in to the water beside them, showering them as I went. They screamed, in what I imagine was sheer excitement. Amy and Rob laughed at the same time as apologising profusely to the boys. I continued to run round and round them in the water and they now joined in my frivolities by flicking water over me, probably to get their own back. I liked 'Cold Water' though!

Along the beach, and in one of the quieter alcoves, we meet a teacher colleague of Amy's with her husband and two children, who were about ten and seven. They were playing down by the tide line, using their buckets and spades to dig a canal that was filling with water, which then led to a moat with sandcastles that they were building. Very similar to the one Dan, Steven and Megan had designed. On closer inspection, the little girl looked like Megan in that she was about the same height but differed as she had a big smiley face - not a moany, whinging face like my human cousin. I flashed her a grin with my pearly whites and out of nowhere, she started to cry. What had I done but pass pleasantries? Amy turned round to see what was going on. I shrugged my shoulders unaware that I had done anything wrong. Boy, could kids be weirdo at times.

To get me out of harm's way Amy instructed me to 'Go play with Coco'. So I ran off and chased her around in the sea and over the rocks. Having had enough of me hassling her, Coco then set about chasing me and we had a massive race along the beach back towards Amy and Rob. Unable to stop in my haste to free myself from her gnashing teeth I ended up running straight through the kids' sandcastles, smashing them to smithereens. I hadn't meant to obliterate them and when I realised I had done so I just kept running for fear of the repercussions.

Mortified by our behaviour Amy and Rob banished us up towards the back of the beach and set about consoling the children by assisting them in the building of even bigger sandcastles than before and decorating them with razor shells and bits of scavenged seaweed. They looked amazing by the time they were finished.

If you thought things couldn't have got much worse, and I am sure that even you couldn't have predicted this, when Amy and Rob next turned around to check what we were up to, it was to watch me sprinting down the beach with a poly bag in my mouth with Coco neck and neck with me, trying to gnash it from me.

"What have they got now?" exclaimed Amy, shaking her head in utter dismay.

"That'll be our lunch," came a curt response from what had been her friend.

I had always had the sharpest of noses and on this occasion it had helped me sniff out these adorable sandwiches nestled between a few rocks high up on the beach, beside some sandals, wellies

a lab report

and rucksacks. Well, I mean, they were just lying there in a poly bag. What happened to the good old picnic hamper with the leather straps to ensure the lid stayed firmly closed and the food safe from flies and dogs? Well, there had been no flies on me that was for sure!

There was a tussle on the beach and the bag burst open scattering the array of sandwiches all over the sand. Rob was now fast approaching, his hands waving from high to low telling us to "Leave them alone." Fat chance of that ever happening when they smelt as good as they did. I grabbed the double decker sandwich nearest to me and pummelled mercilessly up the dunes behind me. Coco grabbed a posher looking one with all the crusts cut off; a girlie sandwich, and followed me up through the reeds and high in to the dunes. The bread slapped off the side of my face as I ran but there was no dropping one morsel of my catch from my pick and nick.

On reaching the top I lay low and started munching my way through my find - it was top smackin' good! I spotted Rob down at the foot of the dunes, hands on hips, shaking his head back and fore in sheer frustration of this stunt. He seemed less than impressed. Perhaps if I had left him a sandwich he might not have been so angry looking. Or should I say, apoplectic or incandescent. Actually, no words could do justice however many I use.

I thoroughly enjoyed my tuna mayo sandwich, which I knew was good for me as tuna and sunflower oil was always added to my tea to help promote a healthy, shiny coat. Coco's sandwich had been even more upper crust than mine, even without crusts, and had smoked salmon and cream cheese on it. The cream cheese still lined her whiskers when we, in a united front, slunk back down the dunes back to our owners.

Rob and Amy's level of embarrassment had reached new heights and I don't think they knew how to deal with this incredulity. Rob meandered down to see Amy's colleague to eat humble pie as a way of offsetting our appalling behaviour (their description of events not ours - we loved our high tea at the beach although there was a lack of water to wash things down). He pushed a twenty pound note in to her hand and asked her to take the kids for a treat on their way home or at least get an ice-cream from the van at the car park. He then skulked off and we were placed on our leads for a very quiet walk home. I guess we had been banished to the doldrums. Even pulling the 'I am sorry face' didn't wash on this occasion as it usually did swing it in my favour. However I still got my tea later on as Amy tried to explain to Rob, who wanted us to skip dinner for being so gob-smackingly greedy, that we didn't understand being punished later on for an event that had happened much earlier; we weren't like kids who could process this type of connection. You bet you I could but liked the concept that they believed that our metacognitive processing couldn't. I could manipulate and mastermind any game in life. What did I say to you about a teacher's children or pets? Proof was in my pudding - or should I say 'sandwich'.

a lab report

22

Agility Training

It was now June, I was fifteen months old and had performed so stunningly well at my obedience training, demonstrating all the basics expected of a silver dog, even as a black dog, I was specially invited to start my agility training.

I was to attend the early session of the evening's training, which was specifically for beginners. Coco attended the later session for competition dogs or those with more experience. I knew it wouldn't be long before I was a member of this group once I had won a few events. Let's face it; if Coco could do it, any dog had the wherewithal to do it. Not that Coco had won that many competitions. She professed that it wasn't the winning that was important but the taking part. That was just her way of processing loss. To me, it was the exact opposite. It was the winning and the taking apart. I lose to no man or their dog!

Training took place every Wednesday evening during the Spring and Summer months. Rob had brought me for my first session tonight and I fully expected to be jumping full height by the end of it. I was already fully conversant with the tunnels, which I could do at break neck speed with my outstandingly agile body. This particular strength or talent had come about from slipping my lead one day when watching Coco, and chasing her through them. This had been great fun and I was super confident at them. I liked venturing in to the unknown darkness. An added incentive for the hard tunnel, which had ridges along it, was that I had heard from various sources that if you were lucky, you sometimes found a dead field mouse you could eat halfway through it, and for that reason I would always offer to go first when we came to this obstacle.

My trainer was called Mary and she would be training me and another beginner, Marney, a border collie, who seemed to have taken an instant dislike to me. Marney's owner had told Rob that for some unbeknown reason she just didn't like black Labs. For some reason, Rob retorted, I didn't like black, white and tan border collies either. It was a lie of course, but one up for good old Rob. I wanted to give him a high five for being so wry but was always wary of giving our game of strategy away. I was secretly impressed though.

a lab report

Mary explained the process of our first few sessions. We would learn how to do backs (left turns) and closes (right turns), which I had learnt to do at my obedience training, and do imaginary jumps between wing stands. I was bowled over with excitement and could hardly contain myself. Next she would be asking my owner to feed me imaginary treats as well but as there was shed loads of bunny poop in the training field, which I could munch on freely between shots, that would not in itself Posie a problem. No wonder Coco was so keen to keep coming to training. Rob had semi-joked about bagging it and taking it home for my tea. Mary had laughed earnestly at such a funny comment. I was less convinced as, being the miser he was, there was probably an element of truth in this.

Mary had set up three jumps in a row, well, pretend ones, and Rob was to run to the outside of the wing stands whilst guiding me through the middle of them on my lead. He was to shout 'go on' at the same time, which was supposed to get me used to running on when he couldn't match my Speedy Gonzalez pace. We watched Marney and her owner go first. The hopeless Collie just spun round and round on her lead, demolishing the wing stands as she went and made no attempt to run between them. She got to go again, and again, and again, until she had made a realistic attempt at trying to get it right. Suitably unimpressed I was now lying on the ground almost snoozing as ten minutes or so had passed while awaiting my turn. Greeedy Collie. Either it was just totally thick and really didn't get it or it was at the ham, so to speak, to get extra shots and make me have to wait for mine. Then again, Collies are not clever enough to be manipulative. It really was the daft leading the daft, hence their affiliation with sheep.

Rob lined me up, after he had coerced me to get back up on to my feet and hyped me up enough to get me interested in jumping. With a 'ready, teddy, go' we were off, at my power walking speed, running between the wing stands until we had completed jump three. I turned round to see if Marney had been observing poetry in motion. Mary praised me and Rob fed me one of my smelly fishy treats from his pocket. It was scrumptious. But then again, so were the bunny poos. Especially the milk chocolate coloured ones, which are allegedly packed more full of vitamins than the dark chocolate ones which had been previously recycled.

Being so impressed by my performance, Mary put the jumps straight up to level one for me, which meant that I was going to have to exert myself to be able to go clear as they were level with my baldy arm pits. To make it easier for me, according to Mary, Rob would jump them with me. This just got better as I would be able to blame him if we knocked a pole down. It was always the handler's fault.

You could have argued it was beginner's luck, but we both managed to go clear. To finish the session, Mary added in one jump to the left of the straight forward ones and Rob had to call 'back' after jump three, so we turned left to finish my circuit over jump four. Hey presto. Me perfecto. I was well impressed by my first session's work and I could tell that Mary had spotted my potential, unlike Marney, who seemed to have regressed as the session had gone on. It was difficult for her to have been paired with such untapped talent as me, who always got things right straight off and

a lab report

with the minimum of effort. I was just so clever.

Week Two onwards

Each week I learned how to negotiate a new piece of equipment and to work on my contacts, which meant making sure my paws touched the yellow section at the bottom of the obstacle before I jumped off or I got five faults. The quality of my contact was aided greatly by a treat being placed there, encouraging me to touch the yellow section to seek it out. Marney had the concentration span of a gnat (insult to the gnat perhaps) and a memory of a sheep and Mary always provided her with short and varied tasks to help maintain her interest and keep her motivated. Often she would run off mid task to give chase to another dog and I would be left hanging about waiting on her returning to her owner so they could finish the course. Sometimes I got fed up with this so when it came to my shot, I would do exactly the same as pay back for wasting my time to see how she liked it. Trial and retribution and all.

The purpose of agility was more than just completing courses over obstacles and demonstrating my speed and dexterity. It was about socialisation, fun, getting a chase, snacking on bunny poops, being fed treats and making Rob look a prat because he couldn't get me to come back to him with any sort of immediacy when I ran amock in the field. Foraging for eats or a chase were always much more fun than performing for Rob's gratification. It was good every now and then to openly show I had a mind of my own and do my own thing; make my own decisions and come home when I wanted, like any adolescent testing the boundaries of their parents.

To return to the original discussion and the trivial issue of me running off, Rob was less than impressed but it got even better than this, as when I did finally return, he was forced into praising me, saying 'Good girl,' when instead he probably wanted to lamp me one. The adorable Mary had warned him that punishing the miscreant, 'me', would result in a no return on future occasions. This was exactly the same as Amy had told him some time ago. Would he never learn! Mary was just the best trainer I could ever have hoped for as, for some reason, she played it that the odds were always stacked in my favour. The term 'Bad dog' was, Mary stated, not to be used to reinforce bad behaviour. Positive reinforcement is what dog training was all about. When I thought about it she is absolutely right. I had never heard anyone say 'Bad human' on my travels. There are plenty of them however.

Over the weeks I learned how to do all the agility equipment; tunnels, the long jump, walkway and seesaw, but my particular favourite was the A-frame. It took me only a mere two sessions to master this piece of equipment. On reaching the top I would linger long enough to use it as my look-out tower to scan for prey. Seconds later I would feel a hand reaching up to prod me and launch me in to my descent, onwards to my next obstacle.

As the months rolled on, Mary was starting to link jumps and agility equipment together to allow me and Marney to gain experience of completing a full length course. This was beginning to get too much like hard work. By nature I was lazy. Bone-idle perhaps more accurate. Making it round approximately

a lab report

twenty obstacles was a huge call. Now, if there had been a hare to chase round it there would not have been a problem as at least I would have been extrinsically motivated. At this moment in time the pending fishy treat just wasn't reward enough – after all performance and food are inextricably linked. A sport psychologist would argue that completing the course should be intrinsically motivating and that in itself should have been a big enough reward. I would argue that is baloney. I knew I could complete the course no problem but, for me, the size and scale of the reward had to be directly equated to the task. Rob would have to work this out over time. Pathetic reward equalled substandard performance; chicken titbits, outstanding performance; fillet steak and some fish treats, winner's performance.

To that end, my first run on a full course was like a demolition derby. Still praised at the end, because he had to, I was given a measly treat. It was my pedestal Mary who eventually suggested to Rob that I might 'work' better for higher level treats like sausage or chicken. It was like night and day when he changed to these. I metamorphosed and became a focused performer immediately. It was amazing the effect that this small adaptation had but it became highly obvious to Rob as one day he forgot my favourite treats and had to borrow some from another handler at the club. He tried to make me work for some stale cheese. That day I did nothing.

During August Mary set up more and more courses for us to get used to doing backs and closes, contacts and tasks involving us running ahead of our owners. Amy came down early one evening to watch me with Coco prior to their training session. I was surprised how much I wanted to impress them and prove how much I had advanced. They stood outside the field's perimeter fence so as not to distract me. I was lined up on the starting line and Rob gave his usual hands up 'Wait' instruction to me until he had walked out next to the first fence he wanted me to jump. I was so busy gazing over at Amy and Coco that my attention was not on Rob so when he shouted 'Go' I never heard him. It took Amy to call on Rob, to get me to look at him, before I followed his instructions. I was hyper with my fans here to watch and to put it politely, I did not perform to the best of my ability. In true commentator style, here's how it went:

"After a slow start, because she wasn't paying the damnedest bit of attention, she's off. She's over the first jump and the second and she's now entered the neck of the tunnel. It's now been ten seconds and there is still no sign of her out the other end. Rob is now peering in to locate her. Oh no. Here she comes, reversing out the way she went in and she's carrying something in her mouth which she's now stopped to eat - her very own pit stop. She's also been eliminated for failing to complete the object the right way.

Never mind, she's back on task. Rosie's demolished the next two jumps and she's now on to the A-frame, and found time in her busy schedule to stop at the peak to admire the view. The crowd are barking her on. She's now negotiated the steep descent, annihilated another jump and is head-butting her way through the soft tunnel as her handler frantically encourages her. She's now re-appeared and is motoring along over the two straight jumps, taking both poles and

a lab report

the wing-stands with her as she goes. The tongue is now out, deep in concentration, as she continues to gain in speed like some wind up toy, racing up to the seesaw and catapulting from its end. She's got two more jumps to go now before her next contact, well she did, but she's decided to run around them and instead is heading straight for the walkway.

She's stopped on the yellow contact. She's stopped for a snack on this penultimate piece of equipment. Is there no sense of urgency in this dog? Rob has now run on to the last jump and is using his hands to beckon her to finish the course. She's on her way, crash, bang, wallop. Rosie's finished her first ever agility course. Well done Rosie."

Rob was walking towards me ready to slip my lead back on and give me, what I believe, merited a substantial treat. Before he had time to do so, I turned around to identify where the persistent clapping was coming from. It was Amy. Using my last drop of energy I ran straight to her and poked my nose through the fence.

"I am so impressed Rosie, Posie," she said, tickling me through the spars.

Coco was wagging her tail and poking her nose through the fence to rub noses with me. I guessed it was her attempt at an Eskimo kiss of admiration for 'an audience with Rosie.' Rob was now attaching my agility lead to my collar, patting my head and offering me three fishy treats. I guzzled them over. That demo should have merited muchus morus.

"She's coming on isn't she," remarked Rob proudly.

Amy looked at him, "Certainly showing promise."

'Promise' I thought. Cheek! I will reiterate the dog is only as good as its handler. In my case however that isn't true. I am undeniably better than mine.

"Mary was suggesting I take her along to the fun day they are having up north in September so Rosie can try a competition given she'll be eighteen months old by then. What do you think? Coco can compete too."

Coco gave a gruff bark. "Looks like we're in too. Should be fun and entertaining at the least."

With my first competition, albeit a 'fun one' looming, I would have to ensure that I was raring to go and ready to entertain the crowds with my talents. Marney, sadly, was not recommended by Mary to go along to the comp with me. It is tough being the best improver in the beginners. When you are a star it is always difficult not to shine too brightly.

a lab report

23

Gullane (Part Two)

It was mid-afternoon on the Friday of the September weekend and it was exceptionally wild and blustery for this time of the year. It had been lashing rain all morning and rather than walk locally along muddy paths and fields, Amy and Rob, who had taken a half day to be able to join us to enjoy an extended holiday weekend, made the decision to take me and Coco to Gullane as the sand is easier to rub off our coats than the dirt. The roughness of the salty sand gives my skin a free exfoliation rather than me spending copious amounts of money paying to have it done at the local spa, called Looming for a Grooming.

On this occasion we had headed eastwards along the cliff

tops to the sweeping, shallow waters at the bay where Coco and I could run in and fetch sticks thrown for us by Amy, Rob, kids or any passers-by that were willing to join in. Coco often managed to find an old tennis ball that had been washed up at high tide or alternatively one she had stolen from some dog less cockily confident than herself. One previous time she had even managed to get a man walking his two gundogs to gift their ball to her through her immense sooking. She would flutter her Coco Chanel eyelashes and men became putty in her hands. Well-admired she was, until I came romping to her side and then the attention and admiration fell to me.

Amy loved photography and always carried her Canon digital SLR camera with her whenever we went somewhere different just in case there happened to be a photo opportunity. Usually that was focused on me doing something extremely crazy or funny; or just capturing my foaming mouth which looked very similar to the froth being created by today's rising tide.

Coco and I raced down the steep brae to the bay and launched ourselves into the water. Even though no stick had been thrown for us yet Coco pretended to look for something deep below the surface and fake how interested she was in retrieving it. I swam on to see if I could chase one of the seagulls riding the waves further out - to my disgust it waited until I was about a metre away from it and flew off squawking or, as Coco told me, laughing at me for thinking I had a hope in hell's chance of catching it. I taunted Coco back saying she must be even more S T U P I D than me pretending to look for something that never existed. I'd say we were now quits!

a lab report

Amy headed further round the bay and positioned herself precariously on some rocks near the lashing tide. Coco perched near her and Amy took her photograph with the white horses in the background. It was whipping up a storm and looked like a Tsunami was brewing. I had seen what the outcome of such tidal waves did after watching a programme on natural disasters with Rob, who seemed to be intrigued by such phenomena. It was through being his tv buddy that I have become the font of all knowledge as I soak up everything I watch like some sponge.

Rob was now standing observing Amy photographing Coco so, as no one seemed to have a beady eye on me, I headed over to the rocks the other way to see what excitement awaited me there. That was when I spotted what I thought was another seagull bobbing about on the water in a rocky inlet; unaware of my presence I performed an Olympic style high dive, similar to those performed in Acapulco, off the edge of my cliff face and into the cold water below. On impact the sea seemed to swallow me up like a shark's jaws as I was engulfed by the waves and dragged below the water's surface, being flung around like a rag doll against the ragged rocks. My head popped up for a second and I gasped for air before I was clawed back under. Where had that seagull gone all of a sudden? Luckily for me and by chance, Rob had seen my head appear then disappear equally as quickly below the waterline, after he had come looking for me when he realised I had done a vanishing act. Shouting over to Amy, who was still busy getting Coco to pose, he alerted her to what was happening,

"Amy, I am going in for Rosie. She's jumped in the water

and gone under."

Without hesitation or a moment to lose, Rob had plunged in beside me, shoulder deep in water, being swept and battered about by the roaring tide, trying to find me in the deep, darkness of the sea. His hands were flailing around in the water desperately searching for me in a blind panic.

Suddenly I felt my tail being gripped tightly and I was being hauled up to the water's surface (the first time in my existence I had been pleased to have my tail pulled by human hands). I coughed and spluttered as Rob supported my tubby tub body, helping my face stay clear of the water allowing me to get a breath in.

Amy was now hanging over the cliff face reaching down to Rob asking him to hand me up to her. He was trying to do so but was so shattered from fighting against the raging torrent of the waves and trying to stay above the parapet himself, he barely had the energy to do this. He just stood still, trying to keep his own footing, holding me close and reassuring me I was going to be alright. Crickey, I knew that. I would have made it without his help - I am sure I would have!

After a few minutes Rob had summoned enough energy in his arms to push me up towards Amy, where I was placed securely back on terra firma. She had taken off her outer jacket and removed her fleece, which she wrapped around me to try and get me a little warmer and drier. She then awaited Rob clambering out of the ravine at the far end; having timed his escape in line with the ebb and flow of the tide, enabling him to get a foot hold in the rocks and climb up on to the embankment. Once out, Amy gave him a huge

a lab report

hug of relief and wrapped her jacket around him as best she could to try to get him warm too; he didn't seem to mind that he was now clad in a pink, girly jacket that made him look more like a Barbie doll rather than Man from Atlantis!

Coco was not very amused by my shenanigans as this now signalled the end of our walk for today as we had to make our way back to the car to get Rob home and out of his wet clothes. I was absolutely fine by now and my coat had started to dry of its own accord after a few vivacious whole body shakes. Why do humans have to wear clothes? Skin dries naturally too. If he had just peeled off his wet clothes and walked in his birthday suit, we could easily have continued on.

As we reached the car Rob took Amy's jacket off and reached into his trouser pocket, extracting a sodden car key and wallet. It was a wing and a prayer that we were going to even get the dog mobile started to zoom us home. I said a quick doggy wish and willed his car's remote to work when he pressed the button. Hey presto - it did. We would soon be home and dry so to speak!

On the way home in the car, Amy had rebuked Rob for being so silly as to put his life at risk by jumping in after me - who had jumped in after the seagull, who had gone in after the fish, who was in the sea after the plankton... I don't know why he swallowed a fly... Perhaps he'll die. I liked that nursery rhyme - sorry, it just sprang to mind as Amy droned on.

Rob loved me and wouldn't have seen me drown; neither would she if she had been in the same position so this was rich coming from her. He told Amy his reaction was instinctive and that she had been right, he hadn't thought through the possible consequences of his actions - all he knew was I was going to drown if he didn't get in there beside me and fish me out. However, Amy rightly pointed out, many owners go in to save their dogs and end up drowning, whilst the dog survives.

"Point taken," Rob remarked to prevent the discussion becoming an argument.

In order to lighten the situation a little, which would be good I thought, Amy recounted a story a pupil of hers had written about his two year old black Labrador. The boy and his mum had taken their dog to the beach and had been throwing a stick in to the sea for it. On one occasion, instead of retrieving it and bringing it back to them, as the stick seemed to have sunk and the dog couldn't find it, it just kept swimming further and further out to sea until it was little more than a dot on the horizon. After calling endlessly for it and trying to entice it back to shore they eventually realised they were on a hiding to nothing and the dog was now well out its depth - in all senses. In sheer desperation and ultimate panic they had used their mobile phone to dial the police to seek advice and support. The police had then contacted the coastguard who immediately sprang in to action to rescue the dog - which they did by sending out a jet ski to pick him up; after putting him in a doggy buoyancy aid they sped him back to land.

How cool did that sound? Most people paid a fortune for a go on one of these - he got a shot for free. Me and Coco giggled like Muttley and Scooby Doo in the back of the car, having

a lab report

understood every word of the story as told - unbelievable as it sounded but true as it had been covered by the local press. It was absolutely hilarious when I took the time to visualise it at the same time as humming the theme tune to Hawaii Five-O.

The only regret I had was that I had not been beach side, in real time, to witness the drama unfold.

j s carle

24

My First Agility Competition - A Fun Day

I was on the start line and raring to go in my debut agility competition in late September. I was adorned in my black and pink spotted collar which was my special agility attire and was supposed to help get me in 'the zone'. All eyes would be on me. I wanted to leave a lasting impression on the onlookers who had paid so much for the privilege of seeing me perform.

"Ready, teddy, go," enthused Rob who sprinted away at top speed towards the first barrier. I dug my claws in, gripped the ground and pushed off, trying to match his effervescence. He was more like the potassium in the water bath and me more like the lead, in terms of my reaction speed. Over I went, clearing it

a lab report

by millimetres. Off we headed to the second jump, which Rob ploughed straight in to, knocking both the wing stands and pole down, sending him flying to the ground at the same time as I had taken off on all fours to jump what was now an invisible barrier - just as well we had practised this at training. I ended up landing square on him like a sack of potatoes.

Instead of just picking myself up and continuing with the rest of the course, I clambered to my feet and started jumping up and down on his back, as he started to sit up, getting more and more hyper by the second; I thought what had just happened was extremely amusing and obviously so did the crowd by the sound of their loud laughter. This wound me up even more and I started licking his face, ears and pinning him to the ground to stop him getting up. What great entertainment agility was turning out to be.

When Rob eventually managed to push me off and find his feet, he got hold of my collar, steadied me to try and calm me down, looked in my eyes and told me we were going to continue and finish the course. With another 'ready, teddy' to get me off and running, we raced towards the next jump, which I cleared no problem, before being coaxed through the weave with my favourite smelling fishy treat (only allowed because it was a 'fun' competition and I was a beginner).

On completion of the last pole, I got a second or two to gobble this over. Lip smacking good... we were off again, another jump which then led us straight on to my favourite obstacle, the 'A frame'. For a dog like me, this was like climbing to the top of Everest and being rewarded with a momentary rest to take in the breath-taking three hundred and sixty degree view, before descending the other side.

Having now reached this elevated position, the peak of my obstacle, I scanned my surroundings. And that's when I spotted it in all its glory: a hen, pecking around on the grass just outside the ring. The light bulb went on in my head, just like with these cartoon characters when they have an idea, and then without a bye or leave, I launched myself off the top of the frame and flew out the ring to give chase! Within seconds, a highly coloured, flustered and embarrassed Rob was high tailing it after me. Some of the spectators gasped in horror, others were laughing uncontrollably, perhaps in disbelief or, alternatively, elated at getting a full-on comedy in front of their eyes. Whichever it was, they were all watching me - I was now starring in my very own floor show, which I am sure was much more entertaining than my performance had been so far in the ring!

I was running full pelt towards the hen, trying to grab its feathers as it tried to peck my face, body, or in fact any part of me it could reach, in order to defend itself. With this being an unsuccessful tactic, it had now changed its game plan and had stopped still to face me up. We then performed a dance with each other - shimmy to the left, shimmy to the right (repeat) pounce forward and gotta ya. But I didn't - so I reverted to Plan B - put my left paw in, my left paw out, in, out, in, out, pluck a feather out, I did the Hokey Cokey and I turned around, that's what it's all about see - Oh hennie, hennie, hennie, oh hennie, hennie, hennie... I ducked and ran off at this point as Rob took a swipe at me trying to snatch

a lab report

my collar. Unsuccessful in his quest, he recruited Amy's assistance,

"Amy, call Rosie and start running in the opposite direction"

"Rosie, Rosie... come... Rosie, come!" Amy shouted frantically as she ran backwards.

The worry in her voice amused me, but in all honesty, it sounded like someone whispering my name in a dream as my mind was still fully focused on tonight's tea.

It was now a good thirty seconds since the chase had begun and Rob had not managed to even get close to catching me through any of his rugby tackles (given he hadn't managed that when I was weeks old there was little chance, in the big scheme of things, that he was going to manage now I was at my physical peak at a year and a half old). Amy had not managed to summons me either so Rob thought it wiser to plough his energies in to securing the hen in his arms to put a stop to this public show down. Bending down low, he popped both his hands under the hen's belly, and swept it up in to his arms, away from my gaping mouth. Darn! Game over.

Amy marched over towards Rob, who did not have my lead on him as we had left it on the start line (agility dogs are supposed to be so well trained there is supposed to be no need to carry the lead with you for such eventualities as had just occurred. The idea is that you just pick it up on finishing the circuit with your under control dog). She held up her hand at me and gave me a 'stay' command. I watched, eyes widening, as she approached me, and just as she closed in enough to grab my collar, I gave my wild eyes look and then darted off in fear of my life.

I ran back in to the ring, high up on to the walkway, and

stood right at the top of it staring out across the course and all the spectators. I saw Rob hand the hen over to Amy, who proceeded to place it gently back over the wired fencing it had jail-breaked from. Besides one or two ruffled feathers and a smattering of my slavers, it looked pretty intact.

Rob raced in to the ring and came to rest alongside me on the dog walk. In order to get me to dismount, he had to be encouraging towards me, 'Good girl', and encourage me down to the bottom of it and onwards to complete the last two barriers to the cross finish line. Which I did. He then slipped my lead back on and patted me, rather too firmly, on the head as he had to be seen praising me in front of the clans. Great manoeuvre by me I thought, to get out of a serious row and another BD comment. The crowd applauded rapturously. What a show I had put on for them.

You will be surprised to learn that I was taken straight back to the car after my event. For some unknown reason they decided not to run me in my second event, which would have been an all jumping round. This was quite a downer given how far I had travelled to be there that day. They seemed exceptionally biased towards Coco who was allowed to do all three of her events. They must have thought that one event was probably enough for my first outing as all the thinking through commands had tired my doggy brain.

On the way home in the car I had a moment of quiet reflection. I was now exceptionally well known for my first appearance on the Grade One circuit. What a clucking good time I had just had. I could really get to enjoy this agility lark (or hen)!

a lab report

As I write I am awaiting my opportunity to attend my second agility event which, alas, will not be until next summer when I will be the grand old age of two years and three months - and still be in Grade One. Rob and Amy made a joint decision not to enter me for the most recent show which Coco competed in and won a third place trophy. They thought it wise for me only to attend in the capacity as spectator; to watch to see how it is done by those in the know. Hmm-mph! I know what to do on all the equipment. It was that hen's fault for goading me from the sidelines and making me lose my concentration. I was blameless!

The best part of coming along to observe Coco in action was not only barking at the participants and watching the agility itself, but being afforded the opportunity to visit the stalls around the side of the course. There I was able to partake of some biscuits, or should I say, many biscuits, going a begging at one of the stalls. They had kindly positioned a ginormous bucket full of biscuit bones just at nose level. I assumed, given their accessibility and close proximity to mouth height, they were either free or alternatively of the pick and nick variety. Apparently not, and I had been totally misled, as when Rob spotted me grazing on them he reacted immediately by hauling my lead in an upwards direction, lifting my nose sharply out of the bucket and causing me to choke on my mouthful. Embarrassed, not for the first time by my behaviour at agility shows, and in order to placate the stall owner, who'd seen me gobble some over, he felt compelled to purchase some more doggy bones for me and pay a contribution towards the ones I had already eaten, or pinched. Strategic and premeditated on behalf of the stall owner if you were to ask me - a good way to form a guilt trip and bring in increased revenue. I would never have coughed up any extra dosh or purchased more having foiled their plan. I didn't perceive it as stealing as they were there for the taking!

To be honest, my act of greed paled in to insignificance against the exploits of one of my compadres who, when attending another dog agility competition, had helped herself to the KFC (Kentucky Fried Chicken dinner to those of you who don't know the lingo) that a family were enjoying. After stealing some chicken legs she had the audacity to return to the picnicking party to help herself to seconds. When her mortified owner had offered to pay for her 'picking and nicking,' the family concerned had been so distraught by it all they had merely ushered her disgraced owner away, packed up the little they had left and scrammed as quickly as was humanly possible. I am sure that will be the first and last time they will ever come to watch a dog show, or if they do, they'll be wiser than to bring such delicious and tempting treats with them. Not that these things are ever the dog's fault - it is always down to the owners. All the books say so.

Agility competitions really were a fantastic opportunity to sample food from around the world, participate in frivolity, chase feathered friends and, as I found out, had equal merit attending in either the capacity of competitor or spectator.

a lab report

25

The Future

Well, that's my life up-to-date. I remain unpredictable in my actions and would advocate that this quality keeps my owners on their toes. They keep hoping that I will mature a bit one of these days. I am not keen to make that day too soon.

I remain a topic of conversation on a day-to-day basis and Rob always receives a blow-by-blow account of my wrong doings on his arrival home. That's probably why he has started to come home later and later. The other day when he came home was one of the best responses I have seen him make to something I had done.

After putting his briefcase upstairs, removing his shirt and tie and slipping in to casual clothes, he appeared back at the kitchen for

Amy to relay to him that George had had to have his legs amputated earlier on that day after a freak accident. I watched as Rob cuddled her in closer to him, gently stroking her hair and inquiring sensitively about what had happened to her Cousin. Taking a fit of the giggles and barely able to speak, she confirmed that it wasn't him she was speaking about, it was George, Coco's monkey. You see, Coco and I had been fighting over him and during our tug of war, had partially torn his legs off and this time they were beyond repair, so she'd had to surgically remove them and sew up his stumps. Unlatching himself from her, he remarked that she needed to get out more as staying at home was obviously having a profound effect on what she thought was important news. He did have a wry grin on his face as he turned away and made the comment, not that Amy could see this of course!

Next month I am going on my holidays. Not that I am actually going anywhere. Confused? Let me explain. Amy and Rob are heading off on Safari to South Africa. I am hoping that they will return home with a real George for me so we can get up to some monkey business together. Rather than leaving me home alone with Coco, they have taken the trouble to arrange for my human granny to look after us - she has been charged with our care. I hoped that is the only thing she will be charged with after two weeks with me. Rather than farm us out to her house, or even worse, to kennels, they thought it best if she came here - damage limitation I think they call it.

Given my human granny has little or no control over me I am excited about the notion of being able to do exactly what I want,